The Mollies Were Men (Second Edition)

The Final Chapter

By

Dr. Thomas Barrett

ISBN: 1-4033-9682-5 (e-book)
ISBN: 1-4033-9683-3 (Paperback)
ISBN: 1-4033-9684-1 (Dustjacket)

Library of Congress Control Number: 2002096056

This book is printed on acid free paper.

Printed in the United States of America
Bloomington, IN

1stBooks - rev. 01/06/03

DEDICATION

"Helene"

Table of Contents

A NOTE OF GRATITUDE

The author is grateful for having access to his fathers old records collected from libraries, colliery offices and newspapers, particularly those of the *Shenandoah Valley Evening Herald*. This book contains legends and folklore, coming out of the past without written memorials often told to our family by my dad. However, it dwells on actual court scenes that are a matter of record.

The author was particularly fortunate to have many friends who encouraged him in pressing on to complete the message and persevere with his father's research over the many years. Three persons were of great value in getting the original job done for my dad: William Sweetland, publisher of the *Shenandoah Valley Evening Herald* at the time the original book was completed. He read the original manuscript and came up with some candid, constructive criticism.

Mrs. Theresa Yodis, society editor of the old Shenandoah *Valley Evening Herald* who read and edited much of the original copy. Professor John J. McGuire: This schoolteacher was personally instrumental in getting *The Mollies Were Men* underway because of a dogged insistence that the "Irish side" was never told. His pats on the back encouraged my dad to no end.

I offer my special thanks to Mrs. Robert (Lorraine Lauritis) Mayefskie. She is a former special education teacher and the wife of my friends and school chum – Bob. She deserves a special place in heaven for having the patience and grit to work with me in getting the grammar correct and making sure I didn't make it impossible for the reader to stay with the story.

My own son Thomas III because he kept reminding me that I better get finished before the history of our ancestors and the pain suffered in the anthracite region is long forgotten. Thomas III always pushed his grandfather and his dad to keep telling the stories that were passed on from our ancestors. He constantly encouraged any story and often asked the right question every time he thought he was being told a bit of Irish blarney.

A special tribute to my wife Helene, for having the push to make me spend the time writing, the patience to listen to the issues I wanted to resolve, and the warmth, love, and encouragement every time I wanted to stop.

God Bless All of You.

Tommy Barrett

FOREWORD

The story you will read might seem to be strange and appear to be a remarkable piece of fiction. It is not fiction. Rather, it is a true story, recorded in the early American courts in Pennsylvania and the small coal mining town's newspapers. On the 21st of June in 1877, in Schuylkill County, Pennsylvania, ten men were executed by court order. All were said to be members of the "Molly Maguires," a secret society formed during the latter half of the nineteenth century by the Irish coal miners of the anthracite regions of Pennsylvania. At the same time there was a fraternal society known as the "Ancient Order of Hibernians," to which most Irishmen belonged. The intermingling of the two groups has a long confused history, although their only proven connection was that all members of both organizations were Irish.

The name, Molly Maguires, is said to have been derived from a woman so named who used physical force against her landed oppressors in Ireland. On the other hand, the Ancient Order of Hibernians was formed to promote friendship, unity, and true Christian charity. There never was a connection made between the two organizations other than several men were members in each.

This story was coming to its end in 1877; one year after the country celebrated the Centennial. Most of the events occurred at the end of the Civil War shortly after the General Lee surrendered. The national theme was reconstruction but the reconstruction was aimed at rebuilding the south. At the same time in the coal country of Pennsylvania miners were being forced into reduced wages, longer hours, unsafe conditions, and blacklisted because they were trying to organize a labor movement. Ironically, the slaves were being freed in the south but the coal miners were being enslaved in the north. The Molly Maguires, according to history, was organized for the planning and execution of a concerted program of physical violence against those whom the miners considered their oppressors, including mine company owners and company executives, and the special "police" under their control.

After going through a wealth of authentic records and doing very intensive research, there is enough evidence to contend that the Mollies did exist. It would also appear that they did perpetrate some crimes. The trials and arrest recorded in the news of the day as reported here show that they were ridden with perjury, false accusations, and unbelievable miscarriages of justice, all condoned by the politicians of the era and those in their employ.

It might take another manuscript to explain the conditions that the miners were working but I provided a Glossary that will help give the reader a better understanding of the conditions. The Bibliography is provided to list the many sources of material and as an additional list of references for the interested reader.

After one James McParlane, a Pinkerton detective hired by a mine executive, infiltrated a Molly "lodge," he carried out a course of espionage among its members that resulted in the conviction and execution of a large number of Molly Maguires. Although several of the Molly Maguires did take the law into its own hands, it is the author's belief that this secret group, was forced to do so by the circumstances of the era and, by so doing, helped to set the pattern for our modern-day enlightened labor conditions in the coal industry.

The trials of the accused men were a travesty on justice. The prosecuting attorney was General John Albright, a mine operator's attorney and Franklin B. Gowen, President of the Philadelphia & Reading Coal and Iron Company, the countries first powerful coal trust company. Gowen never tried to hide the fact that he was out to destroy any effort to organize. He was often quoted that he was determined to smash all organized labor activity in the coal region. History records the "Long Strike," as it came to be known as ending in June of 1875. Miners were forced by hunger to give in and to accept a 20 percent cut in wages. Leaders of the union were compelled to leave the area. Gowen admitted in a report to his stockholders that he spent four million dollars to break the strike, but he argued that the money had been well spent because he had rescued the company "from arbitrary control of an irresponsible trade union."

There were twelve murders for which the Mollies were brought to trial. The earliest date for these murders was in June of 1862. The last came in 1875. Seven murders occurred after the Coal Company hired a private investigator and gave him instructions to run down the bandits no matter how long or how much it costs. The agents instructions from his superior, Allan Pinkerton in part were, "you are to remain in the field until every cut-throat has paid with his life."

The agent named Pat McParlane took the name James McKenna and worked his way into the confidences of several mining groups. He eventually joined the Molly Maguires, became the secretary for one division because he was able to write, unlike most miners, and soon he began assisting in planning murders. Through his own admission in court, he was directly involved with the planning of the seven murders and possibly assisted in getting some of the participants to the crime scene in at least one case while he was on the scene. The only collaboration he had were the words of confessed murderers, James Kerrigan and Manus (Kelly the Bum) Coll, both of which were never indicted. Several others became state witnesses and were set free with no charges filed.

At the same time several of the witnesses for the defense, including women, were sentenced to 30 months in jail for perjury. The trials were conducted in an atmosphere of open hostility against Irish Catholics. The judge in Jack Kehoe's trial was an old political enemy and did not allow key witnesses to testify. No one was either Irish or Catholic was permitted to serve on any of the juries. They were hanged and persecuted, convicted and executed – but they did accomplish their purpose, which was to someday force better working conditions for their fellow man.

We will never know how many were innocent and unjustly accused as the secret group did not speak out, only those that were expelled from the society spoke out and pointed to others to gain their own freedom. In the end, none of the men who decided to speak out, were members of any group. It was a known fact that not all members of the Ancient Order of Hibernians were Mollies, but all Mollies were members of the AOH and, in the final analysis – all the real *Mollies Were Men.*

Chapter 1

THE BEGINNING

With caps down low and collars up high, seven men sat about the circular wooden table in the rear room of the Dead Man's Gully café. The only sound came from hushed voices in the bar outside the closed door.

Seven slips of paper were folded and dropped into an overturned derby in the center of the table.

No one spoke. A man standing in the shadows touched a seated man's shoulder, and this man reached into the derby and removed one slip of paper. The man at his left followed suit and this continued until all seven men had a slip of paper in his clenched hand.

Six of the papers were blank. The seventh contained a sketch of a coffin and dagger, scribbled crudely with a pencil.

Two men got up immediately and walked through a rear door into a garden. One stood up and stretched his arms toward a hanging kerosene lamp. Three remained seated. The seventh went into the bar and ordered a beer. After sipping the drink from a schooner, he leaned over the bar and opened his folded piece of paper. It contained the *Coffin and Dagger*.

He was the man selected to *get rid of an inhumane mine boss*. The Coffin and Dagger was a warning to *get out of the region or accept a dagger that will lead to a coffin*. This was meant for the official who had posted a notice at the mine entrance: "**No Irish Need Apply**."

The man in the shadows who held the derby and slips of paper was not identified. Some 'Irish' researchers feel reasonably sure that he was a Coal Company Cop in disguise.

According to tradition, this dramatic system was one of several used by a group of desperate Irishmen called *Molly Maguires*, who lived in the anthracite fields of Pennsylvania during and immediately after the Civil War.

The scene depicted in Dead Man's Gully, a café near Shenandoah, was repeated in two other sections of the region on the same night. Still according to tradition, the three men who picked the *Coffin and Dagger* would meet at a point announced by the "Body Masters" of each division. The number of men on *an assignment* varied, with records showing as many as six chosen for some jobs.

Much has been written about the Mollies and almost all of it roundly condemns them as vicious murderers and men of evil, who transformed the coal region into a valley of fear.

Some historians claim there never was a Molly Maguire organization. They believe groups operated separately in a half-dozen counties, but also recognize the possibility that there was some collective action through the entire area.

The records do show that there was an organization. James McParlane, a secret agent operating under the name of James McKenna, became secretary of the Shenandoah lodge.

Records also make another controversial point clear; the Mollies and the Ancient Order of Hibernians were two separate and distinct organizations. When McParlane was initiated into membership it was the Molly Maguires and not the AOH.

Final proof is that twenty men were hanged as Molly Maguires. Ten were executed on June 21, 1877, marked as Black Thursday by the Irish of the region.

The name Molly Maguire came from Ireland. One authority traced the origin back to 1843, when the Irish sought to intimidate bailiffs against the collection of house and cattle rents.

The name came from a legendary Irish women of great ferocity, bearing the name Molly Maguire, who showed little mercy in dealing with the land agents.

Some sources claim the original band of Irishmen in the anthracite region met at the home of a women called Molly Maguire. One source, with apparent little foundation, noted that the Irishmen wore female clothes when dealing with their enemies.

4

Although members of the Mollies were referred to as the AOH during the court trials, the only connection between the two units was that "not all members of the AOH were Mollies, but all Mollies were members of the AOH."

The aim and purpose of the AOH was to promote friendship, unity and true Christian charity. The benevolent AOH was recognized as an arm of the Roman Catholic Church, until it was condemned in the region by the hierarchy of the Church.

The action was taken because of the notoriety given to the Society by the public and the press and by the statements issued during the court trials.

Attorney Guy Farquhar, a Commonwealth lawyer, referred to the AOH during a court trial in Pottsville, Schuylkill County, in August of 1878. In part the lawyer said: "This organization, founded in the old country, was brought here by emigrants from Ireland. In this country the Order is composed of what is known as the National Delegates." Attorney Farquhar said the national delegates had a State organization in each of the different states, a county unit, and local divisions of lodges. "The organization was created ostensibly for a beneficial purpose, and it was intended that its objectives and purposes should appeal not only to the benevolence but in the patriotism of its members. But, in fact, at least so far as this coal region is concerned, the organization is a band of cutthroats and assassins who have stopped at nothing for the purpose of carrying out their plans."

The lawyer was wrong. The AOH at no time and in no way was ever proven connected with any crime; yet it was his statements and others like it that prompted the Catholic Church to disband the divisions in the anthracite region.

Since Mollies were members of the AOH it was only natural that they would set up their organization with delegates, divisions, lodges and body masters similar to those in the AOH.

Why did Irishmen, known down through the ages for their delightful wit, laughter and song, and a contagious sense of humor, become vicious and violent?

There had to be an explanation – a reason – for such a profound change in the make-up of a man, especially one reared to love and fear God and keep His commandments.

Self-defense justifies murder. Does this mean only when your life is in immediate danger? Was an Irishman defending his life, his family, and his right to work and live in peace and with liberty? He was blackballed at every colliery because of his nationality and religion, at least for some time. When he did get a job it was backbreaking work.

Records for the period show he worked sixty hours a week and saw the light of day only on Sundays, or during slack working time. He got fifty dollars tops per month for his work. In many instances he was paid in scrip and bobtail checks, good only in "Pluck Me" company stores. He lived in company-owned shacks and was treated by company-employed doctors. His son had no formal education. In 1870 one-fourth of the mining personnel in Schuylkill County consisted of boys from seven to sixteen year of age. Family groups worked together, and when there was a fall of rock and coal, or an explosion, the male members of entire families were wiped out.

In 1870 the State passed a law making the minimum age twelve years for boys working inside a mine. There was no minimum age limit on work above ground. Boys aged seven and eight years were carried to work on the backs of their fathers.

The mine worker bought his food and supplies from a "Pluck Me" shop, with the money deducted from his pay before he received his paycheck. It was the same with his rent and doctor bills. There were no workmen's compensation payments or death benefits of any kind.

If the miner protested, he was laid off and his credit was stopped. History records a worldwide depression in 1870. Flour sold for $5.00 a barrel, but was $6.50 in the "Pluck Me" stores. Butter that sold at 20 cents per pound to the public was listed at 28 cents in the company-owned stores.

Boots used by minors sold at $2.75 cash but were $4.50 "on the book" in the company stores. Eggs were 20 cents per dozen, but 30 cents in the "Pluck Me" shop.

In addition to the long hours and low wages, the danger of sudden death was always present.

The Avondale disaster claimed the lives of 110 mine workers on September 6, 1869. According to the colliery records, nineteen of those who perished were under fourteen years of age. To save transportation costs the coal breaker had been built directly above the mine shaft. It caught fire. A fan outside the mine was started and this eliminated any chance of survival. It drove the swirling clouds of smoke and flame down the mine shaft. The disaster shook the world. Messages of sympathy came from overseas. However, no one was charged with murder, in this mass slaughter. In fact, there is no record of anyone even being arrested.

The mine shaft was the only opening into this mine. The disaster prompted the passage of legislature requiring mine owners to have two openings leading to the surface. It took such disasters to improve working conditions in and about the coal mines.

The miner soon learned that the only other means of improving his lot in life was to organize a labor union. But unions were smashed as quickly as they were formed. In desperation the mine workers laid down their tools in the final week of 1874. The strike went on for six months. The Workingmen's Benevolent Association was destroyed.

Scabs called "Black Legs" were brought into the region to replace the striking miner. The Governor dispatched a militia of 500 men into the coal fields "to maintain order."

Miners and their families survived on huckleberries, wild fruit and vegetables grown in their gardens. Many families also had chickens, cows and pigs.

The long strike was over in six months, but at an estimated cost of $4,000,000 to the coal companies.

While every member of a labor union did not belong to the Molly Maguires, every Molly was a member of the labor union.

Franklin B. Gowen claimed he was a friend of the working man, yet the passage of time makes it clear that this man did more harm to the cause of labor than any other individual in the history of the anthracite region.

During the Molly Maguire trials in Pottsville his defense of the workingman was worthy of any great labor leader; "I yield to no man living in the respect and admiration that I pay to the workingman. Let him who will erect an altar to the genius of labor and I will worship at its shrine, I stand here as the champion of the rights of labor."

He came in the coal region from Philadelphia on April 28, 1856. From the minute he set foot in the coal fields things got progressively worse. At the age of twenty-six he was elected District Attorney of Schuylkill County. He controlled and directed all trials. He selected counsel to prosecute all cases. He attended the hearings and prepared the evidence. He looked after all the details of the trials and the manner in which they would be conducted. Gowen was described as being forceful, courageous and daring, with a personal magnetism that proved well-high irresistible even when his arguments were obviously preposterous. He was also labeled "the biggest hypocrite in the annals of the county." Some students of history brand him "an evil man."

Historical records show that Gowen, instead of being a friend of the workingman, was the ace of all capitalistic persecutors of labor. He was an optimist with an unquenchable craving for the limelight. Large meetings were called just to provide him with an opportunity to make a brilliant address and to feed his egotism on the plaudits of his supporters.

As prosecutor he played on the passions of the community. Here is a quote from Gowen in court: "Oh, think once more upon your own county, almost one vast sepulcher where rest the half-buried bodies of the victims of this infernal order. Victims whose skeleton hands, bleached by the sun and by the wind, are stretching up from out of the thin covering of earth that wraps their bodies in all the eloquence of silent, beseeching prayer, to have mercy upon their fellowmen.

"Oh, solemn judges of the law, ministers in the temple of justice, robed for sacrifice, I bring before you this prisoner and lay him upon your altar. And trembling at the momentous issues involved in your answer, I ask, will you let him go?"

Newspaper accounts of the trial of the Mollies said Gowen had the jury spellbound. Verdicts of guilty in the first degree resulted, in some cases, with less than an hour of deliberation. Every act he staged was for effect. Even his death was theatrical; he committed suicide in 1889.

Tired, dirty, and hungry, the coal miner heads for his home. He saves chunks of bread crumbs for his children. Someone tells him they are good for a sore throat. His mine can contains sulphur water because it can cure corns. There is a piece of pie in his smock, given to him by his working buddy for his wife. He meets his unemployed neighbor, who is also on his way home. He is carrying a quart can filled with huckleberries, picked from a laurel-embellished mountainside.

These men are killers! These men slave by day and slaughter by night!

Hardly. But they are strong men, men with deep convictions. They accept the responsibility of a wife, and usually a big family. When someone blocks the roadway he uses to provide for his family, he becomes aroused. When he is hit he fights back.

When Gowen became president of the Philadelphia and Reading Coal and Iron Company, these men soon had their backs to the wall.

Gowen cut wages, brought in scabs, hired strikebreakers, created the "Coal and Iron" police by getting a State law passed and more than once "maintained order" with the State militia.

Looking back on the "Dark Days," an aged Irishman was quoted as knowing, through some strange supernatural source, that Gowen was nothing more than "a heap of ashes in hell, where he belongs."

Mine unions were organized for survival and the Molly Maguires for vengeance. Bloody pages of history depict the stained hands of Irishmen. Men were murdered, and some Mollies did confess. Such facts are made clear by historians. They are not only made clear but also clearly emphasized. The degree of guilt on the part of those who drove these men to deeds of violence and murder is not made clear. In fact, this is seldom mentioned. God-fearing, patriotic Americans, they organized for their own protection. They were certainly justified in seeking work.

The Workingmen's Benevolent Association was formed. It was smashed by the merciless Gowen. In 1874 the anthracite mineowners arbitrarily refused to renew the agreement with the association. The man behind the refusal was Gowen. He dictated labor policy to all the coal operators because he was the head of the largest mine colleries in the anthracite district.

The first six months of 1875 were a fearful nightmare. All mining operations were shut down by a strike. Railroad cars were overturned and trains derailed. Engine crews were stoned. Many incendiary fires were recorded. The strike marked the end of the Miners and Laborers Benevolent Association, a union founded by John Siney, of St. Clair.

Gowen became president of the P&RC&I Company in1870 and in four years he had secured 100,000 acres of land and invested $40 million to monopolize the anthracite industry. The last thing he wanted was a mine union.

Gowen later admitted in a report to his stockholders that he had spent four million dollars to break the strike, but he argued the money had been well spent because he had rescued the company "from the arbitrary control of an irresponsible trades union." [1]

John Siney, a highly respected man, called a mass meeting of working men in Frackville one night. The next day fifty-five railroad cars were overturned. Although it was rumored that the Mollies were guilty, it was obviously the action of men aroused the previous night.

Gowen had another scheme. He brought a secret agent into the region. James McParlane, alias James McKenna, was twenty-nine years old when he arrived in Port Clinton, Schuylkill Co., on October 27, 1873. He was in the employ of the Pinkerton Detective Agency of Philadelphia. Gowen, consumed by a passion for power, had gone secretly to Philadelphia to arrange for the agent.

An Irishman, McParlane came to the region to betray his

---

[1] Phillip S. Foner, Professor Emeritus of History, Lincoln University, Pennsylvania, author of the History of the Labor Movement in the United States.

fellow Irishman. He had only a meager education. However, he had not only the detective agency and coal companies on his side, but the public, the press, the police, the government, and above all the money.

The glamour, mystery and excitement that go with the secret agent character might be given McParlane by some historians, but not the Irish. They regard the Pinkerton agent as a despicable informer who betrayed a trust and was more guilty than the murderers. One observer said that the detective was not only pretending to be one of us, but became one of us and then turned on us.

During some of the murder trials it was noted that, as secretary of the Shenandoah Chapter, McParlane knew who was marked for murder and did nothing to stop it.

A native of Ireland, McParlane came to America in 1867 and joined the Pinkerton firm in Chicago in 1871. He arrived in Shenandoah in February of 1874, posing as a fugitive he went from bar to bar and made an impression as a counterfeiter. He danced the Irish jig and was a good storyteller, enriched with the Irish brogue. Al of this enabled him to gain the confidence of the miners and just two months later he was accepted into Molly Maguire membership. Soon after this he was named secretary of the Shenandoah lodge.

As a lodge officer he knew every member. He memorized every password and secret gesture of the Division. He not only knew the plans of the Mollies, but also took part in their preparation. Yet with all these advantages, it took him three years to get a conviction.

Attorney Martin L'Velle, who defended accused Mollies, argued that McParlane did very little to prevent crime.

Part of the script:

Atty. L'Velle: Did you indirectly assist in the crimes?
McParlane: I seemed to but it was not a fact that I did.
L'Velle: Did you or did you not? I want an answer.
McParlane: Of course I did not, so far as I was concerned; so far as the members were concerned, they thought so.
L'Velle: Then you were not the party that Jack Kehoe authorized to get the men to kill Bully Bill Thomas; Were you or were you not?

McParlane: Certainly I was.
L'Velle: Did you deem that participation?
McParlane: No, I went down for the purpose of finding out what they were going to do.

* * * * * * *

Ten Irishmen were hanged on June 21, 1877, six in Pottsville and four at Mauch Chunk. The six men executed in Pottsville were Thomas Duffy, Thomas Munley, James Carroll, Hugh McGeghan, James Roarty and James Boyle.

Father Daniel I. McDermott was there. The condemned men were Roman Catholic; all had been to confession.

The priest said, "I know beyond all reasonable doubt that Duffy was not a party to the murder and I think the same remark will apply with almost equal force to Carroll. "I do not want to shield these men nor condone any faults they may have committed, but there are many things bearing upon their guilt that could be explained away with satisfaction." The priest made it clear that he was not breaking the seal of the Confessional. He said he met the men on routine parish calls and on occasions outside the church after services.

The four men executed in Mauch Chunk were Alex Campbell, John Donohue, Edward Kelly and James Doyle.

All convictions were appealed to the State Supreme Court and from there to the State Board of Pardons. Attorney S. A. Garrett, on behalf of the defendants, said to the Board: "I say that from 1876 to 1877 there was not a fair trial in the county."

On March 25, 1878, Patrick Hester, Patrick Tully and Peter McHugh were hanged in Bloomsburg, Columbia County.

On March 28, 1878, Thomas Fisher was hanged at Mauch Chunk, Carbon County.

On June 11, 1878, Dennis Donnelly was hanged in Pottsville.

On December 18, 1878, John "Black Jack" Kehoe, the King of the Mollies, was hanged in Pottsville.

On January 15, 1879, James (Hairy) McDonnell and Charles Sharpe were hanged in Mauch Chunk.

On January 16, 1879, Martin Bergen (Birgin) was hanged in Pottsville.

On October 9, 1879, Peter McManus was hanged in Sunbury, and this was the last of twenty executions.

Chapter 2

A SERIES OF MURDERS

The King of the Mollies was a highly respected leading citizen of his community.

Jack Kehoe was high constable and was county delegate in the AOH. His arrest was personally ordered by Gowen on May 5, 1875, and the charge was assault and battery with intent to kill.

His appeal reached the State Board of Pardons; on April 5, 1878, the Board of Pardons announced it would not interfere. However, in September the Board reversed itself and allowed argument. The final vote was two against two, a tie. According to law this meant the application was dismissed.

There wasn't an Irishman on any of the juries that convicted the Mollies. Several sources were quoted as stating that the trial of Jack Kehoe represented a "most serious miscarriage of justice." During the trials several witnesses were arrested on charges of perjury. Any testimony given in contradiction to the prosecution's testimony would involve the witnesses in a legal action.

No attempts were ever made to rescue any of the prisoners. All remained calm, unlike hardened criminals at the gallows. They carried themselves honorably, many of them quietly protesting their innocence, but causing no undue commotion.

It is a tradition that in a secret band of murderers, even the slightest suspicion of being an informer means instant death. Kehoe could have killed McParlane on many occasions, yet he never made or ordered such a move.

In spite of all the violence over a period of a dozen years there was no show of force during the trials.

Lawlessness was by no means confined to the Mollies. The Sheet Iron Gang and Modocs became involved on numerous occasions, yet none were ever convicted of any crime. However, seven defense witnesses for the Mollies got jail sentences for contradicting Commonwealth testimony.

Historians believed it strange that it took thirty years to smash a small band of men of little means and influence. The first record of a Coffin and Dagger warning was in 1848. It was reportedly signed; "One of Molly's children."

The first murder officially blamed on the Mollies was on June 14, 1862. Frank Langdon, of Audenreid, was beaten by five men. He was a "ticket boss" at a large mining operation. He died two days after the beating. It took place in the midst of a labor dispute. During a strike the sheriff started the water pumps. An angry mob overpowered the workers. The sheriff telegraphed to Philadelphia for assistance and 200 troops were summoned. Order was quickly restored.

Several slayings attributed to the Mollies took place during such riots and colliery strikes. (The Mollies were blamed for the Cass Township Rebellion in October of 1862.)

They were blamed for defying a state draft for Civil War replacements, yet records show that the Irish were well represented among Union volunteers.

Records also show that the Glen Carbon Guards of Cass Township marched to war on the heels of the renowned First Defenders. The Irish were fully represented in two of the county's famous regiments; the 49th and 96th Pennsylvania Volunteer Infantry Regiments.

There was trouble, however, so much in fact, that the President, Abraham Lincoln, sent a secret message, in code, through the governor's office. In essence, the message noted a desire to have the law obeyed, but in an emergency it would suffice to make it appear like it was being obeyed.

Reports of incidents were often based on opinions rather than fact. A mob of 200 men took part in a riot at a colliery and a quoted report stated, "It seems to have been a movement originating in Cass Township where a secret association termed the Molly Maguires exists." Note that phrase; "It seems . . . . ."

In 1863 there were fourteen murders recorded in Schuylkill County and the same number the following year, with twelve more listed in 1865. One was the brutal killing of David Juir, a superintendent of the Foster Township Colliery. It was never solved. He was shot down by five men on August 25, 1865.

The murder of George K. Smith was among the prominent deaths of the time. This slaying took place on November 5, 1863, at Audenreid where he owned and operated a mine.

On January 10, 1866, Henry Dunne, of Pottsville, a mine superintendent, was murdered by five gunmen. It was the first of five murders in the county that year.

In the first three months of 1867 there were five murders, including that of William Littlehales, superintendent of the Glen Carbon Coal Company. He was shot to death outside his home on March 15.

There is a legend concerning this murder. The mine official's eyes were shot out of his head. The Mollies allegedly believed that the eyes of the victim retained the last vision before death and this could be photographed.

In the cold light of historical review, wasn't it odd that the murderers did not have the same fear in other reported slayings?

Henry Johnson was murdered in Zion Grove by a half-dozen men on March 23, 1867.

On October 17, 1868, Alexander Rea, of Mt. Carmel, Northumberland County, was riddled with bullets. The mining official was carrying a payroll to the colliery at the time. He was ambushed. There was no doubt that the motive was robbery. Three Mollies were hanged for this murder in 1878 at Bloomsburg.

On April 15, 1870, Patrick Burns was slain near Tuscarora in Schuylkill County. He was a mine foreman.

Morgan Powell, of Summit Hill, Carbon County, was slain on December 2, 1871.

The Frank B. Gowen colliery, near Shamokin was burned to the ground in 1872. A school teacher in Centralia, named J. J. Green, had both ears cut off. It was said he spoke openly against lawlessness.

Newspapers headlined "A Wave of Terror." All crimes were attributed to the Mollies. They were blamed for produce stolen from farms in the Ringtown Valley. Breakers were dynamited; mines were blasted shut; colliery offices were robbed; timber yards were set ablaze.

Down through the years such incidents were the mark of labor-management strife; but it was not the case at that time. All were blamed on the Mollie Maguires.

The fact that the Irish controlled a solid block of votes was looked upon as some type of mysterious crime. Historians, in most instances, said they were Democrats, yet in 1872 the Mollies were credited with helping elect John F. Hartranft, a Republican, as Governor of Pennsylvania.

Press releases and subsequent books made it appear like it was wrong for the Irish to elect commissioners in both Schuylkill and Carbon counties. It was considered a scandal when the Mollies were quoted, in times of need, as saying: "The Old Man in Harrisburg won't let us down."

On August 14, 1874, Gomer James was charged with the murder of a Molly. The young Welshmen, Dutchmen and Germans organized to fight the Mollies. Two other such groups were recorded in the files of the times; the Sheet Iron Boys and the Iron Clads.

Gomer James was marked for death and McParlane knew this. Strangely enough, historians said Gomer ignored warnings that came from McParlane because the man was a Molly. Who was better equipped to warn of death than a member of the band planning it?

On August 14, 1875, Gomer James attended a picnic in Shenandoah. He was shot and the killer escaped.

On the same day Thomas Gayther, justice of the peace of Girardville, was murdered by an enraged man "on a spree." A drinking man with a temper was naturally presumed to be Irish. In any event both murders were attributed to the Mollies.

On October 30, 1874, George Major, chief burgess at Mahanoy City, was shot and killed during a "free-for-all" fist fight. During a subsequent probe, information led to the possibility that he was shot, by mistake, by one of his two brothers. However, it wound up in the lap of the Mollies.

Fred Hesser, night watchman at the Hickory Swamp Colliery near Shamokin, was clubbed to death in the engine room. The Mollies were charged with this slaying that took place on December 18, 1874.

Michael Lanathan was shot in the street at Centralia and Thomas Dougherty was murdered on his way to work. Although both murders were "shrouded in mystery" the public branded the Mollies as being the conspirators.

On July 6, 1875, Benjamin Yost, chief of police at Tamaqua, was shot down. On September 1, Thomas Sanger, an inside boss, and William Uren, a miner, both of Raven Run, were murdered.

Directly or indirectly, the press and public blamed all of these killings on the Molly Maguires.

Soon after the murder of John P. Jones at Lansford on September 3, 1875, three men were apprehended. It became the initial Molly trial in Carbon County. It started in Mauch Chunk on January 18, 1876.

The first trial in Schuylkill County opened in Pottsville on May 4, 1876, for the murder of Benjamin Yost. Subsequent trials went on for a period of two years. All ended in convictions of first-degree murder.

Trials in Columbia County began on February 8, 1878. All convictions were appealed to the State Supreme Court and all were denied.

Although McParlane claimed he was under suspicion as a secret agent between the time of the arrests and trials, action by the Mollies do not substantiate this. When Alex Campbell petitioned for a new trial the Mollies selected McParlane to raise defense funds. There was no record of any illegality when McParlane tried to reach a judge to have action on the appeal delayed. He raised $200.00 and turned it over to Jack Kehoe's wife.

The court proceedings on the appeal were strictly private, yet representatives of two newspapers were allowed to attend as "a special courtesy." Campbell based his appeal on the "tampering of the jury" but his appeal was denied.

McParlane was on the job over three years, and was a trusted member and officer in the Mollies. He knew all its secrets and yet it took three squealers to convict the Mollies.

Kehoe was tried three times. It was common knowledge that Gowen was "after the King." He knew if he got Kehoe he would be the coal tycoon, heading a $25,000,000 yearly business. He took a leave of absence as head of the big coal company to assist the prosecution "without pay."

James Carroll, James Roarty, James Boyle and Hugh McGeghan were tried for the murder of Benjamin Yost. This started on May 4, 1876, and the very next day Gowen ordered the arrest of Kehoe. He was charged with assault and battery and intent to kill. Kehoe, father of six children, was convicted and got from five to twenty years.

The second charge was conspiracy to kill William and James Major, brothers of George Major, who had been murdered. Found guilty, Kehoe got another seven years in jail. This was still not enough for Gowen. He got his "real break" not from his agent McParlane, but from a Molly squealer. Michael "Muff" Lawlor implicated Kehoe in the killing of Frank Langdon. Lawlor was first deputy of the Mollies in Shenandoah at the time. This was enough for Gowen to have Kehoe charged with first degree murder, although the slaying took place fourteen years before this.

James Kerrigan, another squealer, was indicted for the murder of John P. Jones. He was in jail nineteen months and was then set free. Edward Kelly and James Doyle were arrested with Kerrigan for this murder. Later Alex Campbell was arrested as an accessory. All three were hanged.

Any doubt about the miscarriage of justice was wiped away by the third squealer. Three men were executed for the murder of Alexander Rea, yet a fourth man who confessed went free.

Manus Coll was called Kelly the Bum and that he was. He was convicted of highway robbery in 1867. When the defense questioned the testimony of a criminal who never served his full sentence, the prosecution presented a pardon.

The court records will show that Kelly the Bum admitted firing the first shot at Rea "into his skull." He also admitted taking money and a watch from the dead man's clothes. He named three colleagues.

On March 25, 1878, Patrick Hester, Patrick Tully and Peter McHugh were hanged for Rea's murder, yet Kelly the Bum was never indicted.

A legend, with little foundation but much significance on the subject of "Justice," is contained in the tale of a captured Molly.

The Sheet Iron gang met at Fiddler's Green on Broad Mountain. The Molly lost his way and strayed into the camp. He was nabbed and immediately tied to a nearby tree and told to "make your peace with God, as you'll be burnt to a stake in the morning."

Meanwhile a priest, on a sick call, was attracted by the bonfire. The bound man called to the clergyman and quickly made him aware of his awesome plight. The priest summoned the gang and protested.

After a hushed conference, a spokesman in the group announced that the Molly would get a "50-50" or "sportsman's chance" for his life. Two cards would be presented to him at dawn, one marked "Life" and the other "Death." His survival depended on his pick. A guard on duty just before dawn, whispered to the Molly: "My conscience bothers me. You don't have a chance. Both cards are marked Death."

At sunrise the cards were placed face down on a tree stump, overlooking a swirling stream of water that disappeared quickly into wild, thick shrubbery. After a glance at the back of both cards, the prisoner suddenly reached out, picked up a card and threw it into the creek. In a moment the card was caught up in a twisting current and disappeared. The Molly turned to the priest and his captors said; "That card in the creek is mine. If the one on the stump is marked Death, the one I picked must be Life.

Tradition has it that Lost Creek got its name from this incident.

Fantastic? How much more fantastic than the known developments of the time?

Scores of men were murdered, yet the twenty hangings involved only seven slayings. The others went unsolved.

Did Gowen and the government, the press, police and public, actually want justice or the heads of the Mollies?

Published tales referred to mobs and gangs with hundreds marching on collieries and through communities, yet the Shenandoah lodge of Molly Maguires, on McParlane's own records as secretary, consisted of only forty men. Such vague testimony as "they looked like Irishmen" was accepted from prosecution witnesses.

The *New York Times* was quoted as saying the Pottsville jail was "absolutely impregnable, except through the assault of an organized army aided by artillery," yet most of the court records of the trials were stolen or "removed" from this very courthouse.

In more than one instance priests and defense lawyers called the trials "a miscarriage of justice." Were the records removed because of this? The attorneys for the Mollies included John W. Ryon, a congressman, Linn Bartholomew, Martin L'Velle, S. A. Garrett and W. P. Ramsey.

One of the most renowned cases was the execution of Thomas Fisher[2] at Mauch Chunk. The condemned man vigorously maintained he was innocent. He placed his open hand on the wall of Cell No. 8, which had been newly plastered, and said the imprint would remain there forever, as a supernatural sign of his innocence.

The mark was there at least until 1931. That's when the *Philadelphia Bulletin* said, reporting at the time that it was scraped off by an irate official. Tourists at the jail swear they've seen it since.

Martin Bergen was given a reprieve of one month. It came minutes after he was hanged.

---

[2] The open handprint on the wall can still be seen in the jail cell in Jim Thorpe, Pa, formerly known as Mauch Chunk. There is still some debate about the legend. Some say it was Alex Campbell that put his hand on the wall but the local press and the Philadelphia Inquirer printed stories in March of 1898 that it was the supernatural sign that Thomas Fisher left to proclaim his innocence.

When Patrick Hester was hanged, his widow placed a gold ring on his body. It was stolen, but returned ten days later, with a letter to the Sheriff signed by the thief. Historians find no record of this man being arrested.

Kelly the Bum had been a Molly. When pardoned, press releases pointed out it was not established whether Governor John Hartranft pardoned the Bum because he had been a Molly. Wouldn't this imply he was a Molly sympathizer?

The reprieves were granted – the one that came too late and another for a youth named John O'Neill, who was convicted with Hester O'Neill, got life.

Captain Robert J. Linden, of Philadelphia, worked with McParlane. The officer would arrest McParlane on raids and then get him alone for reports. Then McParlane was set free on lack of evidence or on some other pretense. Wouldn't an organized band of murderers become suspicious? In spite of this constant contact and protection and firsthand knowledge of developments, it took three informers to bring results. It certainly made it appear like

McParlane was either a poor agent, or there wasn't too much to report.

Many of the slayings took place after men were fired from their jobs, when mines shut down and when wages were cut. Although the Mollies represented only a small segment of the working force, they were blamed for the action of the whole.

Often heads of a colliery organized the workers themselves. The miners were sent to other collieries to cause enough damage to hamper and halt production. This was a means of eliminating competition.

On February 3, 1866, a Pottsville newspaper demanded that coal operators blacklist anyone known to be a Molly. Another county publication advocated "lynch law." It considered the law unfit to cope with secret organizations and a hindrance to swift justice. What was just about lynch law?

Muff Lawlor's bar, prior to the time he became an informer, was destroyed by a mob. There was no one arrested although public reports stated that Tom Hurley was "almost lynched."

A mob of about fifty men marched on the home of Charles O'Donnell in Wiggans, near Shenandoah, on the night of December 10, 1875. He was not home. A son, however, was riddled with a half-dozen bullets and a daughter was also slain. A coroner's inquest concluded the deaths were at the hands of persons unknown. They are still unknown.

Wasn't it rather odd to say that a jury consisted of no Catholics "so it would not be influenced by sympathy?" By this same reasoning, wouldn't it be true that a jury of non-Catholic would be biased?

Letters to newspapers from workers made it quite clear the dispute was between management and labor and not just Mollies.

One letter historians revived pointed out that the worker was "robbed" of thirty per cent of his wages, but the coal companies "lost forty per cent of their profits because of it." The writer said he was against shooting, but with the union smashed the only defense for the working man was his gun. He also noted that not only one nationality, but all nationalities were paid only fifty cents a day.

One Coffin and Dagger note had this message attached: "Any Blackleg who takes a union man's job while he is standing for his rights will have a hard road to travel and he will have to suffer the consequences."

After the trials Gowen was quoted as saying the industry "had rid itself of the last vestiges of trade unions."

One poet acknowledged defeat with the following poem:

"Well, we've been beaten, beaten all to smash,
And now, sir, we've begun to feel the lash,
As wielded by a gigantic corporation
Which runs the Commonwealth and ruins the nation.
Our wages now grow beautifully less
And if they keep growing thus, I guess
We'll have to put on magnifying specs
To see the little figures on our checks.
It's nothing strange to find on seeing the docket
That we've worked a month and nothing in our pocket

It makes a man feel dirty, cheap, you bet
To work a month and then come out in debt."[3]

The most solemn and sober thing about life is death. It is particularly so to the survivors of those condemned to death. There is dishonor and disgrace; the mourning heart overflows with sorrow.

Yet on the morning of the four hangings in Mauch Chunk, eight cavalry troops of the Easton Group paraded through the streets, led by a drum and bugle corps. "Nero fiddled while Rome burned."

For an entire week before the six Mollies hanged in Pottsville, an undertaker had six coffins in his display window with the names and measurements of the six condemned men inscribed on the caskets.

Gowen, however, was an actor. One of his touching moments was his response to the cries for mercy by the orphans and widows.

---

[3] Attributed to Joseph F. Paterson. Last Secretary of the Workingmen's Benevolent Association; the poem is paraphrased from a popular miner's song at the time of the great strike in 1875.

Gowen said, "If I close my eyes I hear voices against which you cannot close your ears and which are pleading for mercy. Oh, so strongly that my poor words are but empty as the ear. I hear the dying sufferer cry, with his crushed face turned up to the sky. I see him crawl in agony, to the foul pool and bow his head into its bloody slime and die."

This was the man who offered a special gift to the miners for Christmas in 1874. They got "bobtail" checks, layoffs and their credit was stopped. Instead of getting Santa Claus they got the state militia, with fixed bayonets for toys. Gowen called the Mollies "infidels, atheists." Yet the condemned went to confession and received Holy Communion at a Mass celebrated in the prison.

In spite of his talent and training, McParlane went on for over three years as a secret agent, amid scores of murders, without results until one man became an informer.

He courted Mary Malloy, a sister-in-law of James Kerrigan, who became an informer. What better source of information? He lived in Fenton Cooney's home in

Shenandoah and was befriended and trusted by Frank McAndrew. These men, both Mollies, would hardly keep secrets from the secretary. He mixed and mingled with Mollies in all the bars, this secret agent. What happened to the traditional loose tongue of the drunk? He knew about a mob marching on Simon Trier's shop in Mahanoy City. It ended with a murder that McParlane apparently did nothing to stop. He was there.

A man of Polish descent, Anthony Cheracovich, was badly beaten. He worked with Mollies and not Modocs. The detective did nothing about any arrest in this incident.

McParlane telegraphed his messages and sent others into the post office, yet he was not suspected of being a spy for over three years. It is hard to believe the Irish hadn't a friend in the post office. The detective apparently had the support of seven priests and a bishop. One of the priests, Father Daniel McDermott, was on a sick call at Jerry Reilly's bar in Heckscherville. Mr. Reilly's daughter got out the horse and wagon to take the priest back home. On the way they were waylaid and the wagon overturned. They walked miles to their destination. No one was arrested.

Reilly and his customers retaliated. They went to Pottsville and wrecked a bar. They were arrested. Any wonder there was resistance, retaliation and even rebellion?

An accessory is one who helps in an unlawful act. One Molly asked, "Isn't an accessory to murder one who provokes it?" He was depicting the detective as an accessory to murder and violence and therefore as guilty as the one who actually committed the crime. During some of the trials the defense tried to prove that McParlane was an accessory.

There is no doubt that the law was broken and murders committed by frustrated, bitter, resentful men. Twenty men paid the price with their lives. They went to their graves, some confessing, others protesting, but all with a prayer of forgiveness to all.

What happened to those responsible for the inhuman working conditions? What was their degree of guilt and punishment? Was their conscience anything like the message on the grave of one working man?

"For 40 years I worked with pick and drill,

Down in the coal mine against my will.

The Coal King's slave, but now it's past,

Thanks be to God, I'm free at last."

Chapter 3

AUNT MAMIE'S RECORDS

Patrick Mulrooney kissed Marie Swartz. At that moment she became his queen. Awkward, immature, without any class, the kiss, nevertheless, carried an impact that shook Pat's inner being. Its stimulant was in not being rejected or repulsed. He was accepted!

Her bare feet dangled from the narrow wooden bridge that spanned Lost Creek. Her toes touched the rippling surface of the shallow stream. The water sparkled in the light of a full moon.

Mulrooney was a man resurrected. He experienced a sudden elation, a resurgence into a new, enchanting world. He was in love – and sixteen-year-old Marie was his queen!

Marie felt a similar emotion. It was evident in her flushed face. Her empire was in the heart of this senior high school student. To Mulrooney her hair was no longer sweeping folds of tinted brown. With the birth of love, it was transformed into sparkling strands of shining jewels. The dark hills, with twisted birch, shaggy laurel and stalwart pine silhouetted against an immense sky, suddenly became a kingdom for a newborn queen. Off in the background, on a knob of rolling clay and solid rock, stood the castle of a queen, no longer a wooden, drab, two-story gray, wooden structure.

The staccato of chirping crickets became a rhythmic sequence of appealing sounds to a young man's ears. Later, much later that night, they kissed again at the garden gate outside the Swartz home and exchanged a hushed goodnight.

———————————

"But, mother, I love her."

"Love her! What do you know about love! You say love when all you mean is lust."

The remark left Pat crimson-faced, "Mother, please!"

"Please is it?" She put down the stove lid. "What do you know about the Swartz tribe? They hate the Irish. It was the likes of them that hanged your grandfather."

Pat put down his schoolbook. "Now, Mother, how can you blame Marie Swartz for what took place years ago to the Molly Maguires?"

"Who else am I to blame? Your dead father, may he rest in peace, and his father before him will turn in their graves." She pointed an accusing finger at her son, "Sure it's hexed they have you."

A knock on the kitchen door broke the mounting tension. The shrill voice of Katie Murphy, a robust neighbor, called from outside.

"Mrs. Mulrooney, it's raining. You better take your clothes off the line."

A swift sweep of a strong arm, and a shawl was removed from the back of a wooden chair. Circling her head with it, Mrs. Mulrooney hurried through the kitchen door. Pat reached for a wicker basket on the floor nearby and followed quickly on his mother's button-shoe heels.

Huckleberries were plentiful that year. Marie told Pat about a "kutch" near the parish grounds in Lost Creek. It was a beautiful day in mid-June when the unpretentious young couple sauntered up through Duck Street.

They trudged up a winding pathway to a clearing bordered profusely with thick shrubbery. Marie carried an open dinner pail, with a handle made of twine attached to holes made near the top of the oblong container. Pat held a drinking glass in his right hand; his left rested on Marie's right shoulder.

"What do you know about the Ku Klux Klan, Pat?"

"Nothing much, I know they are no good and they hate us Catholics."

She smiled. "Last night they burned a cross outside the Wild Cat Cemeteries. I went there because of a legend."

"What's a legend?"

"Well, it's like your church traditions. It is history out of the lost past. You know old Mrs. Zimmermuth, the witch. She told me I would see the face of the man I will marry in the flames of the cross."

"You don't believe that stuff, Marie. That's a lot of baloney and hogwash.

She squeezed his arm. "You know what, Pat? I saw your face. Honest to God, I saw your face."

Pat grinned, "Well now, maybe there is something to it."

It was just after Pat spilled his second water glass of huckleberries into the dinner pail that an insect landed in his left eye. He winced.

Marie shouted, "Don't rub it, Pat. Come on, we'll go down to the home of the witch. She's a powwow. She has ways of getting it out."

Mrs. Zimmermuth, known throughout the mining region as Aunt Mamie, lived at the foot of the hill. Pat sat in a chair in the kitchen of her home, his hand over his left eye.

"Hold his head, Marie," the woman said. She leaned over Pat, gently removed his hand and placed a long, sharp tongue in the young man's eye. The action surprised him, but he sensed relief in a moment.

Mulrooney looked up into the face of this strange woman. He saw lines of age in a gaunt, scraggy countenance, yet he was impressed and flabbergasted. He saw a fading beauty in the lean, hard face. He knew her as a repulsive, hideous witch with unnatural powers of sorcery, but he was looking into the eyes of a kind, gentle old lady. The voice was soft and soothing and not the shrill, cracking sound he expected to hear.

Sweat poured down his checks and he felt hot, feverish. Aunt Mamie filled a tin cup with a steaming liquid from a pot on the kitchen stove.

"Here, young man, drink this."

He had heard about these bitter potions, prepared by this woman. This stuff would cast him under her spell; he would be hexed. She was a powwow, a conjurer who summoned evil spirits by an invocation, or some strange magic.

Taking note of his hesitancy, Aunt Mamie extended the tin cup.

"Don't be afraid. This is seasoned with a combination of herbs, flavored with the sap of trees and blossoming flowers from your huckleberry mountain."

Mulrooney looked helplessly from the woman to Marie and back again. Marie was running her hand over the back of a black cat that appeared from beneath a nearby chair.

"You want to hex me," he said bluntly. "I heard all about you. And you, Marie. Are you part of this devilish scheme?"

"Oh Pat, be quiet," Marie said. "She is just a nice, harmless old woman who tries to help those in distress. She wouldn't hurt a fly. Drink it; it will do you good."

Love conquered fear. He took the cup in his one hand, held his nose with the other and gulped down the liquid. It was bitter and made him cough yet it was warm in his stomach.

"There's just a drop of whiskey in that," Aunt Mamie said, "but it will be good for you. Sit back now, and rest a bit."

"Look, there's nothing wrong with me," Pat said. "I'm grateful to you for helping me with my eye. But I just don't believe in witchcraft or superstition."

Aunt Mamie walked over to an old desk and placed her hand on a book. Marie picked up the cat and sat in a rocking chair.

"This is the Bible," the woman said. "You do believe in the Bible, I read passages from this biblical record. And I read prayers from it and it helps people."

"You see, Pat, she has helped you," Marie said. "My father said there would be a sign and wonders and Aunt Mamie is an instrument of such powers."

Aunt Mamie turned from the Bible, her one hand still resting on its open page.

"Mulrooney, this may startle you, but I too am a Catholic. I am a granddaughter of the real Molly Maguire."

A lokey whistle pealed piercingly across the Lost Creek Valley. The chugging of a struggling engine through the Colorado Cut aroused chickens roosting in coops along New Road. The hissing steam from a leaking valve at the Hammond Colliery went unheeded by dozens of men in overalls and mining caps. They were pleasant sounds to all in the mine village, as it meant the colliery was working a double shift.

Mulrooney and Marie were with Aunt Mamie in the attic of her home, taking books and papers from trunks and wooden boxes.

Armed with the old records, the three descended narrow creaking stairways into the kitchen and sat around a square, wooden table.

"These newspaper clippings, colliery records and notes on the Molly Maguires were saved by my grandmother," Aunt Mamie said. "They are records you will not find in the county court, because they were lost or stolen. Your search for the truth is at hand."

This had become a passion with Mulrooney. He saw those records as facts, unvarnished or changed by time. He was grimly determined to make his own records from these books and papers, "even if it takes all summer."

They agreed to meet and take notes one night a week. This strange trio would compile the facts and perhaps keep them for use as a thesis later in college.

Mulrooney developed a strange fascination for Aunt Mamie. He said once to Marie: "She grows on me."

On his visits to her home he learned that Aunt Mamie's grandmother had given birth to a daughter, Mary, who married Claude Zimmermuth. Aunt Mamie was born to this couple. Her mother died in childbirth and her father was killed in a mine explosion. It was from her father that Aunt Mamie learned of the eccentric customs and powers of the medicine man. Crumbs from the double-decker mining cans mixed with green fodder, or herbs and sap taken from birch trees, were boiled together to produce a concoction that would cure whooping coughs and sore throats.

She used sulphur water from colliery streams to cure bunions, arthritis and rheumatism. She tied handkerchiefs and ribbons around the heads of her patients with headaches "to keep the bones from separating." Children with fever and inflammation drank her bitter medicine.

And with it all she quoted passages from the Bible, seeking divine guidance in her work.

This purported magic did not impress Mulrooney any longer. He considered it all absurd, a superstition without any credulity; it was foolish and of no perceptible value.

But this woman had what he wanted – the key to the truth about the Molly Maguires. Marie would help him; she loved him. Together they would bring out the truth about the Mollies.

It was not until they were finished with months of research that they agreed on a title for their records. They called it: "The Mollies Were Men,"

The creek bed was reduced to a mere trickle on a hot summer evening when Aunt Mamie and the two young lovers began to compile the Molly records. Collieries in the area were working only two and three days a week as the hot spell dropped the demand for coal.

Aunt Mamie pulled her long skirt about her to avoid "sticker" bushes along the pathway between her kitchen and the chicken coup in her back yard. Mulrooney and his girl were sorting notebooks, newspaper clippings and colliery records on the kitchen table.

A boy with flaming red hair peered through a paling fence and shouted, "Quack, quack, quack." He waved extended arms up and down, mocking the action of a flat-billed waterfowl.

Aunt Mamie ignored the mimicry. She was thinking of the two young friends inside her home. Would they have the fortitude needed to complete the immense task before them? Would the many distracting influences of youth divert their attention from this work? She fervently hoped not. Her decision to "open the books" was prompted by the apparent interest on the part of the two lovers and by their opposite views. She saw contrary interpretations of the records, but was convinced their affection for each other would overcome any bigotry. Perhaps this was the way to learn the truth. Were the Molly Maguires as bad as their enemies said and continued to say down through the years, or as good as their Irish relatives insisted?

Aunt Mamie removed an apron, sat down at the table and said, "Well, kids, let's go."

Mulrooney used an open-end tablet from school to record the material.

* * * * * * *

The date was March 11, 1876. Edward Kelly, Michael Doyle and Alex Campbell were prisoners in the Mauch Chunk jail. At the same time James Boyle was locked up in Pottsville. All four were facing murder charges.

An artist was engaged by a newspaper in an attempt to get portraits of the three prisoners at Mauch Chunk. A reporter known to Doyle visited the prisoner to see if he would object to being sketched.

The reporter asked, "Doyle, I have a favor to ask of you. I want you to give me some facts connected with your life."

Doyle replied, "Well, I don't care about speaking about myself as I suppose you want to put it in the paper, and until I lose all hope, I don't want that to be done."

The reporter continued, "Now Doyle, I want you to consider for a moment. I can find out all about you anyway, but I would very much sooner have you tell me, as then I can depend upon you having the facts."

After thinking it over for some time, Doyle was quoted as saying, "Well, all right. I suppose I might as well tell you, but you will have to put it in proper shape."

Doyle drew the visitor's attention to his legs. Upon each was a handcuff attached to a light chain about fifteen inches in length.

Doyle: "You see I am chained, and I would like to let the people know it. I have to sleep in my clothes and think that it is rather hard on a fellow."

He refused to sit for a picture "until I have lost hope, and you know they have taken my case to the Supreme Court."

Then Doyle said: "Surely to God they wouldn't hang an innocent man, would they?" After asking this question he agreed to the portrait.

Kelly also agreed to sit for his portrait. He seemed unconcerned when he said, "If you give me a pencil and some paper, I will write my own life and give it to you."

Campbell was taken to a barber and sketched without his approval or knowledge. It was in the corridor outside the cell.

There was a fourth man in jail, one James Kerrigan. He was arrested on the same charge as the others, the murder of John P. Jones.

The reporter picked up a poem written by Kelly:

"'Twas Jesus, our Saviour who died on the Cross of the tree,
To open a fountain for sinners like you and like me.
His blood is the fountain which pardon bestows
And cleanses the foulest wherever it flows."

* * * * * * *

Mulrooney drank water from a tin cup and offered a suggestion. "Why not follow the daily records and retain the interesting and pertinent parts? This will avoid repetition."

Marie agreed and added, "Surely the notes made the day or day after the actual events took place will be authentic."

Aunt Mamie made it unanimous but suggested adding footnotes as personal views. "It can be like living it again. We are about to take skeletons out of the closet. We hope to uncover proceedings as they were recorded when they actually took place."

On the very day the news of the prisoners in the Mauch Chunk jail was reported, the following also appeared in print:

* * * * * * *

March 11, 1876

"James Boyle is in the Pottsville jail on a charge of complicity in the murder of Police Chief Benjamin Yost."

The news release: "Evil communication corrupts good manners. No matter how pure a man may be, let him but associate with companions beneath him in the social scale and in ninety-nine cases out of a hundred he descends to their level instead of elevating them to his influence.

"Looking at Boyle as he sat facing Kerrigan testify against Boyle, we wondered that if it were possible that such a manly, handsome-looking specimen of manhood could possibly be guilty of the terrible crime of murder, and we concluded in our own mind that if the evidence against him was not simply conclusive that we would be induced mentally to give him the benefit of the doubt, for a more happily innocent-looking face we never saw occupy such an unfortunate position."

Boyle was twenty-four years old and single. Neighbors were astonished by his arrest. He was the best looking prisoner in the county jail.

March 13, 1876

A brief biography of Ben Yost, chief of police at Tamaqua was made public. It noted that he was killed in Tamaqua on July 6, 1875, at the age of 35.

A picnic, held on July 5, attracted large crowds. They stayed late into the night. It was two o'clock the next morning when Chief Yost and an assistant named Barney McCarron attended to the street lamps.

Yost mounted a ladder to extinguish a light. McCarron stood idly watching directly across the street. A shot broke the silence of the night. Yost staggered and fell. He saw two figures run up the street. He fired. The shots were returned. Yost was shot through the back.

On February 4, 1876, six months after the murder, coal and iron police and Tamaqua borough officers arrested Hugh McGeghan and James Boyle of Summit Hill, James Roarty of Coaldale, James Carroll, of Tamaqua and Thomas Duffy, of Reevesdale.

The official and formal charge was complicity in murder.

March 17, 1876

A news release featured a review of the slaying of Thomas Sanger, at Raven Run. He was shot presumably by Mollies on September 1, 1875, shortly before 7:00 A. M.

Sanger was the inside mine boss of the Heaton Colliery operation. William Uren, a miner and friend, was with Sanger at the time.

Five ruffians, as the news release called them, demanded jobs. Sanger said there were no jobs open. The five men drew revolvers and fired. Sanger was hit but tried to reach the home of an outside boss.

He dragged himself to the steps outside the back door. One of the five "ruffians" followed. A few more shots were fired. Sanger reached the door and fell into the arms of Mrs. Robert Wheevill. He died in minutes.

Uren, his friend, was also shot to death.

Scouting parties were organized. Sanger's father was a Methodist minister. Sanger left a wife and six children.

On February 10, 1876, Charles McAllister and Thomas Munley were arrested for complicity in the murders of Sanger and Uren. Warrants were also out for Michael Doyle and James McAllister.

Charles O'Donnell was also wanted. He was taken from his bed on December 9, 1876, by a band of masked men and was shot to death.

William Uren was a son of a school teacher. Prior to this fatal incident he was served with "Coffin Notices." The fatal shot struck Uren near his chest. He was carried to his home by friends and died that afternoon. He was twenty-two. His parents lived in Cornwall and William Uren was one of nine children.

The double murder took place in Schuylkill County whereas John P. Jones was killed in Carbon County. Edward Kelly was the first man indicted in the slaying of Jones.

James Kerrigan became a material witness for the Commonwealth. E. R. Siewers was district attorney in Carbon County and George R. Kaercher was the D. A. in Schuylkill County.

March 27, 1876

James "Powder Keg" Kerrigan was announced as a witness against the man charged with the murders of Jones and Yost. However, Kerrigan was locked up at Mauch Chunk for complicity in the murder of Jones at Lansford on September 3, 1875.

Kerrigan's mother had died in his youth. His father was described as being part of the "brute creation." The man called "Powder Keg" was born at Tuscarora in 1843.

Published notes of that day: "As he grew in years he grew in wickedness. He moved to Silver Creek and lived in a hut. He was ignored by almost the worst characters in the area. His father being broke, walked from Tuscarora to Silver Creek. On the way, one day, he met a log team. He straddled a log when a wagon wheel mounted an obstruction. It jarred the logs and Kerrigan was unseated.

He fell under the wheel, which crushed out his worthless life."

His son "Powder Keg" was depicted as a "reckless character who was not the possessor of a single virtue that is remembered, unless we made an exception of brute courage."

Mulrooney followed the record verbatim: "It was one cold day in the mine. A fire was built and circled by miners. There was no room for Kerrigan. He threw a keg of blasting powder into the flames. Horrified, the men scattered. He reached into the fire snatched out the powder and sat down. After this he was called 'Powder Keg.'"

The records portrayed Kerrigan as a slate-picker with a bad reputation, who became a miner with a decidedly worse one. "A man no one liked and all distrusted."

He enlisted in the Army and served in Company M, Eighth Pennsylvania Cavalry under command of Captain Benjamin Pilfer, and was later transferred to Company D, 16th Pennsylvania Cavalry. He was in the armed forces three years.

Kerrigan married the "stout and large" daughter of George Higgins. They were the parents of one son and three daughters.

"He was thoroughly bad. His appetite for whiskey, good or bad was much larger than one would expect to find in a man of his diminutive size. He was unscrupulous, wicked, a desperado."

Kerrigan entered the Messrs. Landauer and Company clothing store and paid $10.00 for an overcoat priced at $20.00 while Landauer was busy with another customer. Weeks later Landauer saw the coat on Kerrigan and exclaimed: "Barefaced theft."

Kerrigan laughed. "Ah, I was too sharp for you, wasn't I?"

The notes from the public records of the day continued: "While on a ripper Kerrigan tackled Aaron King, of the coal and iron police in Jeddo. King beat him. Kerrigan went into a stable and got a pitchfork and waited. At midnight, he tried to impale King. King saw him coming, however, and beat him with the handle."

Morris Flynn was a tailor with a shop in a hotel at Tamaqua. Kerrigan, accompanied by Thomas Duffy, saw Flynn walk toward the hotel and said, "There goes the Irish tailor from New York."

Kerrigan assaulted Flynn, but the tailor broke away and called for help.

Officer Yost heard the cry and reached the three men outside the locked hotel door. Yost overpowered the two men. While Kerrigan was down, Flynn "amused himself by jabbing a razor he carried in his breast pocket into Kerrigan in the most free and easy way imaginable. Flynn was dragged off by Yost but Kerrigan's face was stabbed to pieces, and it served him right."

Although never trusted by his companions, Kerrigan was cunning enough to worm himself into their secrets. "He has proven himself even more base than his worst enemy ever imagined, but bad as he is, he has conferred an incalculable favor upon this community and upon the coal region."

Mulrooney laughed out loud. "And this is the man whose testimony was accepted in court. This is the man who went to jail for murder and who went scot free without a trial. What a deal!"

On March 28, 1876, a "second" wage reduction was announced. The wages, in the press of the day, were described as being "miserably low." Families faced great difficulties in making ends meet and often failed.

Newspapers called it a depression and one editorial blamed it on "hard money and people in Congress." One Irishman said he readily understood about "people in Congress" but "hard money must mean the difficulty in getting any of it especially from coal operators."

Men moved sluggishly in gum boots through twisted muddy roads. The dirty brown, black-streaked mud sucked truculently at the knee-high boots. Rain and disuse had rusted the tracks through Smoky Hollow.

This was a big day in the coal region. March 28, 1876, marked the opening of the murder case against Edward Kelly. The charge was conspiracy in the murder of John P. Jones.

In checking Aunt Mamie's records the lovers came to an agreement after a heated debate. Mulrooney wanted to follow the records word for word. Marie insisted this would make a mass of material that would be of little interest and no significance.

It was finally agreed that if any one of the three thought a particular note held any interest it was jotted down.

The first point of agreement was that the counsel for Kelly moved for a change of venue. This was based on "undue excitement and prejudice against the prisoner." A second reason was that "bodies of Minute Men were formed to protect the jail and this procedure increased the prevailing excitement."

This was denied by the court. The Commonwealth argued there was no excitement. "The Minute Men constituted a body of men formed to resist the efforts of a supposed organization in favor of the prisoner. The idea of a change of venue is buncombe."

Kelly was taken out of his chains and brought into court. He was *guarded* by seven coal and iron policemen. Someone asked for James Kerrigan. Someone else said separate trials were requested. Kerrigan and Kelly were indicted together.

Counsel for the defense again argued that the presence of Minute Men represented a prejudice against Kelly. The District Attorney said they were all deputy sheriffs. Kelly was brought to the court in a carriage. A reporter managed to get on the seat between the driver and a coal and iron officer. The reporter wanted the life story of Edward Kelly.

The newsman turned and looked into the coach.

"Why, Kelly, I always imagined that you were a man of your word."

Kelly: "Well, perhaps I am, just as much as you are."

Reporter: "What do you mean by that?"

Kelly: "Don't you remember when I gave you my picture that afternoon that you promised to send me up some cigars? You did not do it."

Reporter: "Well, upon my word, Kelly. If I did I forgot all about it. When I left the jail that day I had just time to catch the train."

Kelly: "I didn't know that, but when I found out that you had gone back on me, I went back on you."

A little later in court, Judge Dreher announced that the application for change of venue was denied. "Edward Kelly, you are charged with the murder of John P. Jones at Lansford. Are you guilty or not guilty?"

Kelly, firmly and with conviction: "I am not guilty."

The panel of jurors consisted of sixty names and fifty-seven answered when called.

Christian George possessed no scruples on capital punishment and did not take a great deal of stock in newspapers. He said he understood English, "except the kind used by lawyers." This man entered the box and was the Number One juror.

H. H. Everett was second and Elias Koons third. John Koefer was challenged peremptorily and the next man, John

Stockett, said he would "try to render a just verdict, but I am afraid to trust myself." He was excused.

Similar situations continued in selecting the jury. Edward Rommel said he had no scruples but had formed an opinion and said it would require other evidence to change his opinion. He was challenged for cause by the defense. The challenge was overruled and Rommel was then challenged peremptorily.

Daniel Rex was "too Dutch" and was excused. Although Reuben Snyder was described as being "too Dutch" also, he was accepted. Elias Smith and William Roehrig were acccpted on March 31, Samuel E. Meckes "hadn't" a shade of scruples "against hanging a man." He was accepted.

District Attorney Siewers, in his opening remarks, declared that "for two days and two nights Kelly and others tracked Jones like bloodhounds until at last they shot him down. We will produce witnesses who saw the defendant, with others, the night before the murder."

Kelly's mother was in court, her head bowed in tears.

The D. A. continued: "Do your duty like men, not actuated by the feelings of this sorrowing mother, but by the state of the six little orphans of the murdered man." He was facing the jury but he was pointing to the defendant's mother.

On this same day, March 31, 1876, the newspapers in the region made a big fuss over the "mystery of William Powell." The man disappeared three months before and was last seen at the Merriam Colliery, near Locust Summit.

Powell worked with Michael Melladay and Thomas Canfield. They searched the mine breast. Company officials joined in the search. Mine patches were scoured; coal sheds and shacks were examined. Word was relayed to collieries and police stations throughout the mining area. Word spread that Mollies knew the answer to the mystery. Sensational stories of a mutilated body went by word of mouth and mine patch to mine patch.

William Powell showed up alive and well. He had spent three months in a "poor house" in the Middle Coal field under the sheltering care of the guardians of the poor.

On the same day a poem appeared in print that was written by Michael J. Doyle and given to the turnkey on the 17th of March, Saint Patrick's Day.

William Madara, the turnkey, turned the poem over to the newspapers. It contained eight verses and a chorus and was called: "Doyle's Pastime on March 17." It described in rhyme his food and life in prison.

The chorus:

"Can I walk or can I talk or can I anyone see? No!
But closed up in a dismal cell in hopes of liberty.
So then I sat down, my breakfast for to eat,
For when a man is in good health I tell you it goes sweet.
Now to conclude and finish with one more word to say,
This is a nice way to be on St. Patrick's Day."

April 1, 1876

Edward Kelly, twenty-four, on trial for murder was in the Mauch Chunk courthouse. He lived at Mount Laffee and worked at Mahanoy Plane. A few weeks after his arrest, Kelly's father, John, was killed by a fall of rock and coal in a mine.

Mahanoy Plane was a small mining community, developed along the Reading railroad tracks. Located in a low valley, it was a mile lower than its neighbor to the south, a community called Frackville. To save miles of track and much time, two tracks were erected up the side of the mountain and railroad cars hoisted from the foot to the tip on steel cables attached to an engine house at Frackville. This was called a "plane" and Mahanoy was derived from a family name.

Kelly was surrounded by mine coal and iron officials; three sheriffs and six guards, all heavily armed. Margaret Murphy took the stand. She testified that she saw three men the day before the murder, but knew only one – James Kerrigan. Her husband, William Griffith, saw Kerrigan with "bad characters."

John Evans, a blacksmith, saw Michael Doyle but not Kelly, John Dale, a car oiler, saw two men near the oil house, later joined by a third man. Aaron Hoffman was uncoupling cars on a dirt bank when he saw three men. James McLaughlin, a fireman on a locomotive, saw two strangers in a nearby oil shed.

Mary Davis lived near No. 5 Tunnel and said that three strange men asked her for a drink of water. She asked them if they were looking for work and one said, "Yep." She fed them and one of them paid her two dollars.

Oliver Griffiths, mule driver, met two men at the Lokey House.

William R. Watkins, a miner, said Michael Doyle asked if the miner was paid by the car or by the yard. Watkins said he got $5.00 per yard. Doyle said that "it should be nine dollars."

These witnesses and others established the fact that at least two strangers, and possibly three, were in Lansford the day before the murder.

William R. Watkins took the stand.

General Albright addressed the witness: "Which is Kelly? Is it this one?"

"Yes."

The general was pointing to the wrong man.

It took some time to restore order in the courtroom. The defense was accused of trickery. Kelly's brother was the man identified by Watkins.

William Jones, a miner on the night shift, overheard Kelly say he would like to see the boss for a job.

Abraham Raitline, a timberman, said he saw three strangers on September 2.

"Which one is Kelly?"

Raitline walked off the stand and put his hand on the shoulder of the wrong man. It created a sensation.

Samuel Strauch, a timberman, was the next witness. He pointed. "That is Kelly, sitting there behind Captain Peeler." He was pointing to the defendant's brother!

The defense brought Kelly's brother, John, to the stand.

"Were you in Lansford, or anywhere near Lansford on September second or third last year?"

"No."

"That's all."

_____

The next man to take the stand was David Lawson. He testified meeting two strangers on the colliery slope. Both asked for jobs. Lawson said he could say under oath that the men were Kelly and Doyle.

The next two witnesses said they saw the two men. W. W. Radcliffe, outside foreman, saw them in the Lokey House. Edward Mennig, mine engineer, saw them outside the carpenter shop. He said he heard Doyle say it was a hot day.

John Jones, a youth twelve years old, saw three men. He said, when cross-examined, "I wouldn't altogether swear that Kelly was one of the men I saw."

James McLean, a mule driver, met them on a dirt bank and one of them asked who was boss. He told them. "John Jones, who else?"

M. A. Wurley served them a drink at the Hotel Eagle in Summit Hill at 5:30 P. M. on September 2.

John Whilden said he left the colliery at 5:00 P. M. and saw three men on foot on the wagon road.

Mrs. Elizabeth James, sister of the murdered John P. Jones, lived next door to Alex Campbell. She saw three men between 6:00 and 7:00 P. M. on September 2 and "they looked tired."

Her husband, Thomas James, saw them at 9:00 P. M. They were outside the Campbell home. One picked up some gravel and threw it at a window. Campbell came out, talked with them in a hushed voice, and then returned to his home. The men followed Campbell.

April 3, 1876

The trial continued.

Mrs. Anne Faux, sister of the slain Jones, saw Kerrigan a half-dozen times that day at Campbell's hotel.

Charles Kline, a merchant, said he sold a pistol and cartridges that day but could not say he sold them to the prisoner.

The murdered man's wife took the stand. She said her husband left the home at 6:55 A. M. and a half hour later was dead. That was the morning of September 3, 1875.

David Miller said he came upon three men on the street at about 5:30 A. M. on September 3. He put his hand on Kerrigan's shoulder, thinking he was his boarding master. He admitted being wrong and said, "Excuse me."

Isadore Romig was working at the Eagle Hotel on the morning of September 3. He said two men entered through the back door. One wore a hat and the other a cap. The man with the hat drank whiskey and water but the man with the cap drank only water.

Solomon Bachman, a driver, said he saw two men in the alley at the rear of the hotel. He said Doyle was the larger man and wore a cap. Kelly was wearing a hat.

Charles Goslee of Coaldale, swore he saw four men and said he had three drinks with them.

James McKeever was on his way to the Top Plane at 6:40 A. M. when he heard three shots. He saw two men with pistols in their hands and one wore a brass button on his cap.

When cross-examined he admitted being twenty-five to thirty yards away and yet saw a small brass button. He said the men moved along a pipeline and disappeared over a small hill.

John Weyhenmeyer, trainmaster, was turning a switch when he heard a shot, followed shortly by four more shots. He saw two men run to the pipeline. The smaller man, at one point, went down momentarily on his hands and knees. Weyhenmeyer ran toward the man he saw shot and the wounded man fell just as the trainmaster got to his side.

Weyhenmeyer: "My God, John Jones, is this you?"

"Yes."

"Do you know who shot you?"

"No."

Then he died.

When cross-examined Weyhenmeyer said he saw Doyle and Kelly in Tamaqua, "I thought they were the men on account of their clothes. But the small man looked smaller and the large man larger." He said he saw them run for a period of ten to fifteen seconds.

August Belsner, a boilerman, said he heard a shot and saw one man on a pipeline. He was shooting into a nearby brush.

Belsner said, "I thought the man was shooting at a dog. Then I saw a man's hand held up above the bushes. I then heard four more shots. I definitely saw three fired. I ran toward the spot and saw the backs of two men and gave them chase into the edge of the woods."

When cross-examined Belsner admitted the nearest he got to the men was about seventy yards.

Defense: "You saw shots fired at this distance?"

Belsner: "Yes."

David Williams jumped off the lokey tracks when he heard three shots. He saw Jones stagger and fall. He heard Weyhenmeyer shout, "Run after them, Dave." However, they had already disappeared into the woods.

J. C. Kantner was in the telegraph office and heard one shot and then three more.

Joseph McNeil was also in this office and he heard only one shot. However, he saw two men with guns at the pipeline but could not identify them.

Mrs. Daniel Boynon saw Jones near the railroad office. She saw two men pass and thought they were heading for a train to Summit Hill.

Mrs. Anne Williams heard three shots and ran out of her home to face two strange men.

Mrs. Williams: "What's wrong?"

One of the men said, "Nothing."

Mrs. Annie Zprye watched three men for five minutes from her bedroom window on the second floor of her home, but could not identify them.

Mary Haggerty said she was on the roof of the Mansion House in Tamaqua and saw two men on Sharp Mountain for a few minutes but "they were too far to distinguish."

Edward Fibish, a painter, heard three or four shots, but he wasn't sure. He reached Jones before he died. Fibish saw two men but was about 400 yards away and could not identify them.

April 4, 1876

The trial continued at Mauch Chunk.

David Evans, mine boss at the Bear Ridge colliery near Mahanoy Plane, said Kelly worked on August 25, 26 and 27 as a loader at this mining operation. He wanted a job as a "starter."

Dr. Horace DeYoung testified that the wounds were sufficient to cause the death of Mr. Jones.

It was 11:50 A. M. on September 3 when W. S. Allebach saw two men near a spring. He called to them to "halt" but they did not stop.

"I cocked my musket and again cried, 'halt.' Doyle stopped and asked what I wanted. I warned him if he didn't come down I would blow out his brains. He came down and was followed by Kelly."

Later in the lockup Kelly had cartridges and a few pennies on his person and a piece of paper containing the name James Carroll.

Andrew Lindsay found a revolver under a log. He searched the vicinity and in fifteen or twenty minutes found two other revolvers. "From the appearance of the weapons I thought that there was about one night's dew on them."

Wallace Guss saw Kerrigan at the spring. He shouted, "Throw up your hands." Kerrigan surrendered without a word.

In jail Kelly wore a badge marked AOH. It featured a figure representing the sun, a harp and two clasped hands.

In this testimony Wallace Guss and Kelly left Mount Laffee at 5:00 A. M. on September 2, walked to St. Clair and on to Tamaqua. He asked for a job at one mining operation along the way. He met Doyle at Crow's Hollow near Tuscarora. The two men met Kerrigan at the mine shaft in Lansford.

April 5, 1876

In the closing talks for the prosecution it was noted that 110 witness testified for the Commonwealth. Not one witness appeared for the defendant.

"To lie in wait for you victim is premeditated murder. This man is a danger to society. It is not necessary to know that this man pulled the trigger. It is not even necessary that he be near the spot, because if he is a confederate he is guilty. If he was there when Doyle fired his gun and rendered no aid to Jones, he is guilty of murder in the first degree," This for the prosecution.

The defense: "We can find 100 pistols in Mauch Chunk that those bullets will fit. It is a free country and what is wrong with being seen in Lansford or Tamaqua? One witness pointed out the wrong man. Another identified buttons and medals at seventy yards. Still another saw shooting at 500 yards. Testimony has been conflicting, with some hearing one shot, others three and four and even five. Some saw two men; others three and at least one witness saw four. One said he saw Kerrigan looking for goats. Kerrigan owns no goats. I say, as true Christian men, do not allow mere bias carry you away."

April 7, 1876

In his charge to the jury Judge Dreher asked the members to "consider all circumstances."

The jury was out two hours and forty minutes.

Judge Dreher: "Gentlemen of the jury, in the issue between the Commonwealth versus Edward Kelly, have you reached a verdict?"

Mr. George, the foreman: "We have. We find the prisoner at the bar guilty of murder in the first degree."

The jury was polled.

A motion was made for a new trial on the writ of error and was referred to the State Supreme Court.

Christian George, the foreman, said later that two held out for second degree on two ballots. "The third ballot was for either acquittal or first degree."

During the trial a confession was published and attributed to Kerrigan, proclaiming his guilt. Later another article declared that this was without foundation.

April 12, 1876

Kelly was brought into court at 11:00 A. M.

The motion for an arrest of judgment and a new trial was not argued. Kelly was sentenced to be hanged.

The prisoner was asked if he had anything to say.

"No, your honor. I have nothing to say but that I am innocent of the crime of killing John P. Jones."

April 13, 1876

Regional newspapers featured a notice, posted by the South Bethlehem Public Works: "Do one of two things. Sever all connections with the AOH or quit."

According to the articles, twenty-one notices were served to individuals. Only one said he would leave the Order (AOH).

April 13, 1876

Alex Campbell was indicted for participation in the murder of Jones and was locked up at Mauch Chunk.

He was thirty-five years old and married to Mary Breslin and they were parents of a two-year-old daughter. He mined coal for about four years and then entered into the hotel business.

May 1, 1876

The gallows were up for Doyle. He had been convicted at a trial in Mauch Chunk that preceded Kelly's trial.

(Aunt Mamie and her two young historians selected the Kelly trial for their notes, after agreeing both were similar in nature with Kelly's trial being more dramatic. The defense produced no witnesses in either case.)

The gallows were built in spite of the fact that it was learned that the Supreme Court would not meet until March of the next year. There was a widespread clamor for a special session for the sole purpose of hanging Molly Maguires.

During the Kelly trial the Miners and Laborers Union called meetings in Shenandoah. With seven branches from District No. 6 participating, donations were solicited and received for destitute families of imprisoned Mollies.

The money disappeared.

Chapter 4

THE POTTSVILLE TRIALS

Aunt Mamie was wise in the ways of love. She left her two young friends alone. She donned a shawl and walked along the winding railroad tracks to Regan's store for brown sugar and chicken feed.

She could have waited until the next day, but she wanted Pat to have Marie all to himself. She walked along the creek banks and stopped often to watch the leaves flow along the rippling water, stooping as she proceeded to avoid an overhanging willow.

A full moon moved up over the eastern horizon and cast a warm glow over the valley. She was thinking of her notes and clippings.

"This is the night we start on the big trial in Pottsville." She had gone over them many times before. Records no longer available in the county court were contained in her files.

While daily reports of developments might be slanted they nevertheless brought out the facts. Biased opinions could be discerned and rooted up like weeds, revealing untarnished historical facts.

She was surprised to find the two lovers lost in the records. Marie was carefully sorting the mass of material while Pat was copying them in chronological order.

Aunt Mamie pulled up a chair across the table and with an elbow on the table and a hand cupped on her chin, she watched the proceedings.

Pat looked up. "Gosh, this is terrific. It is hard to believe that these things actually happened."

Pat's written account of the records"

May 3, 1876

Headline: "The Great Trial To Begin Tomorrow. The Yost Murder Case. Over 200 Witnesses to be called. A great legal struggle expected. A brilliant array of talent for and against the prisoners."

The lead in the article: "This trial will be far more interesting than was either the Doyle or Kelly trial. These two were altogether one-sided and from the first it was plainly perceived that no defense would be made.

"But in this case it is different. The Commonwealth will present from 70 to 80 witnesses and 127 will appear for the defense. There will be two trials, one for one prisoner and the other for the four remaining defendants."

May 4, 1876

The five prisoners were brought into court by a body of coal and iron policemen. The prisoners were James Carroll, James Boyle, James Roarty, Thomas Duffy and Hugh McGeghan.

Judge Pershing announced, "let the prisoners be arraigned."

The five prisoners were charged with the murder of Benjamin F. Yost, on July 6, 1875.

Judge Pershing asked, "Are you guilty or not guilty?"

All five answered in unison: "Not guilty."

The Judge continued, "How will you be tried?"

Roarty answered, "By God and our country."

The first juror called was John R. Davis. He said, "I have conscientious scruples in regard to capital punishment. I would hang them for killing a man. I have heard of this case and from what I have heard and read, I have made up my mind that they are guilty."

The next man called was Joel Betz. "I don't have scruples in regard to capital punishment. I know nothing whatever about this case. I don't even know what case it is."

"Did you ever read what was said to be the confession of James Kerrigan?"

"I think I did in the *Miner's Journal*."

James Fenney was called next. "I have scruples on the subject of capital punishment. I am against hanging." He was challenged peremptorily.

Next came Lewis Jones of Tamaqua. "I have conscientious scruples on the subject of capital punishment. By this I mean to put the law on them for killing. I don't understand English very well. I would understand the testimony. I have heard of this case and have read about it. I have formed an opinion as to the guilt or innocence of the prisoners and I have it now."

Wallace Guss had an opinion that could be changed by the evidence.

"Do you belong to a society known as a "Vigilance Committee?"

There were objections, and a lengthy discussion. Attorney John W. Ryon, for the defense said, "The parties forming this organization went so far as to hunt up the names of witnesses subpoenaed by the defendants and placed those names upon the books of the company as criminals."

Attorney Ryon re-phrased the question, "Do you belong to an organization whose object it is to detect and punish criminals?"

"Yes."

"Where the members bound by oath?"

"Yes, by an obligation."

"Then you belong to an organization that has for its purpose the punishment of these men who are on trial?"

"Not these men particularly, but the punishment of all who are guilty of murder in this county."

"What is the name of your society?"

There were objections, loud and long, and a debate for the rest of the day.

May 5, 1876

Wallace Guss was called again, but the court decided that he should be excused. The name of the "secret society" was never mentioned.

The next juror called was William Becker. "I should like to be questioned in Dutch as my knowledge is very slight. I am not opposed to hanging."

Attorney Ryon stated, "I do not think this man would understand all the testimony. I think he should be excused."

The court disagreed. A challenge was made by the defense for cause but was overruled by the court. The juror was sworn.

Patrick Reilly, the Irishman was excused.

The panel was exhausted with only eight selected for jury duty. The sheriff called sixty more.

Just before court adjourned for the day the twelve jurors were picked. Not one of the 12 was Irish or Catholic.

The lawyers for the Commonwealth: District Attorney George R. Kaercher, General Charles Albright, the Honorable F. W. Hughes and attorney Franklin B. Gowen. Mr. Gowen was listed as an observer.

Counsel for the defense: General Daniel Kalbfus, attorney Daniel Dougherty, the Honorable Linn Bartholomew and attorney John W. Ryon.

May 6, 1876

(It was announced in court that Jack Kehoe, Michael (Muff) Lawlor and James Roarty were taken before a squire today on a charge of conspiracy.)

The first witness was Mrs. Yost, widow of the murdered man. She saw her husband on the ladder at Lehigh and Broad Street at the lamppost.

"I heard two shots and saw him fall. I ran out and met him on the pavement. He said, 'I'm shot and I'll have to die.' I said, 'Who shot you?" and he said, 'I couldn't tell, but it was two Irishmen' and then I sent for a doctor."

The defense objected to the phrase "it was two Irishmen."

"Objection overruled."

Dr. E. S. Sollidy took the stand and testified that Yost was shot in the stomach, between the eighth and ninth ribs on his right side.

Yost had said to the doctor, "Although they were strangers I saw them last night in Carroll's. I am the wrong man they shot. They were after Barney McCarron."

The doctor had asked Yost if the men were Duffy and Kerrigan and Yost had said, "No, it wasn't any of our men."

The defense asked, "You are positive that Yost said neither Duffy or Kerrigan shot him?"

Dr. Sollidy replied, "Yes."

It was on May 6, 1876, that District Attorney Kaercher called,

"James McParlane."

Everybody in the courtroom looked around. They saw a man they knew as James (Mac) McKenna. There was a rush to the railing.

The witness spelled his name, letter after letter, and it was McParlane. He said he belonged to a national detective agency and came to the county to discover who was connected with an organization known as the *Molly Maguires*.

He said he was sent by Major Allan Pinkerton. He went into detail as to where he stayed in Girardville and Shenandoah. He said he did not remember ever seeing or knowing James Boyle, one of the prisoners.

He had joined the AOH on April 14, 1874 at Shenandoah. He had worked for two weeks at the Indian Ridge mine and six or seven weeks at the West Shenandoah colliery.

He demonstrated the signs and passwords of the Mollies. One he gave was: "What is your opinion of the Tipperary election?" The reply: "I think England broke her constitution by rejecting Mitchell." Another was "Keep your temper cool, sir." The reply: "I will not raise it to my friend."

They changed every three months.

One sign was the forefinger of the right hand in the sleeve of the left arm of the coat and the answer was the thumb of the left hand in the left vest pocket.

Franklin B. Gowen asked the witness if $100.00 was an award offered to a murderer who got credit for it by the organization.

McParlane answered, "Several claimed credit for the murder of Gomer James at a meeting in Tuscarora."

The defense objected on the grounds that a particular act could not form the general characteristics of any organization and the Gomer James murder was immaterial to the trial in the murder of Yost.

The Honorable Lin Bartholomew asked, "If murder was committed by one member of a society it could be inferred that the entire society was guilty."

McParlane answered, "Any member who exposed another who committed a crime was immediately expelled."

Bartholomew continued, "Didn't you say if someone doesn't shoot Franklin B. Gowen that you would do it yourself?"

McParlane replied, "No."

Bartholomew questioned, "Didn't you tell Jack Kehoe you were going to Locust Gap to burn mine cars?"

McParlane answered, "No, I was going to the Gap to find out who was going to burn the mine cars."

The witness said he sent his reports to Philadelphia by mail and telegram.

Under cross-examination McParlane admitted having the pistol that was used to shot Gomer James, but denied saying he would do the job.

"Did you join the Molly Maguires?"

"I was initiated on March 14, 1874, in Shenandoah. I later officiated as secretary and during four county conventions."

McParlane admitted taking part in a parade from Shenandoah to Mahanoy City during the strike in 1875, but denied he was investigating any labor organization.

He said he was present on August 25, 1875, when John Slattery was expelled from a convention for giving out information to a person concerning a confidential matter. Slattery, at one time, was a candidate for county judge.

On Wednesday, May 10, 1876, McParlane was still on the stand. He admitted that Kerrigan offered to send "some good men to Lansford to assassinate Jones."

McParlane furnished one motive when he testified that McGeghan was refused a job by Jones, even though he was arrested for the murder of another man. He also made it known that Yost "almost murdered" Duffy when the Irishman resisted an arrest after a brawl. Yost had also abused Kerrigan as a division master of the Mollies.

Kerrigan had informed the detective that the Yost murder was "a clean job." He said that Carroll had agreed and predicted that the murderer "would never be found out."

"Alex Campbell told me he had prevented Kerrigan from shooting Jones on July 29," McParlane testified "Campbell told me Boyle was present at the murder but that McGeghan did the job."

McParlane also testified that Roarty was afraid to buy cartridges for his pistol, as it was the one that was used to kill Yost. When asked how he knew this, McParlane said Roarty was the man who said it.

McParlane: "I attended a meeting of the Mollies in Shenandoah about the first of September, 1875. It was a special meeting called for the purpose of selecting three men to go to Lansford and shot John P. Jones. I was present and was selected as one of the three men.

"Thomas Munley and Mike D'Arcy were selected and a man named John McGrail of Shenandoah was also mentioned. I suggested that I go ahead. My purpose was to arrange for their arrest, including my own. I got on the train at Mahanoy City. McGrail said he was not ready to go, and he did not go.

"I took the two men to the house of James Carroll and said I wished them to be kept there. Those are the men, I told him, who were picked to shoot Jones. This was Thursday, September first, and I stayed all night with McGeghan.

"I told Mrs. Carroll to give the two men a bed for the night. I wrote my detective report in Carroll's. Munley had received seven dollars for his costs from the Division.

"In the evening I asked Carroll where Kerrigan was and he said Kerrigan had gone to Lansford with two men to kill Jones. It was 10:00 P.M. and utterly impossible for me to save the life of Jones. I knew that Kerrigan had been looking for men, but I did not know that he had gotten them.

"I told Carroll the job had been taken out of my hands. In my own mind I contemplated a postponement of arrangements. I had arranged that Captain Linden should be on the grounds and was sure that Jones would be able to save himself. But a little after 7:00 A.M. the news came to Tamaqua that Jones had been shot."

Defense: "Why didn't you warn Jones?"

McParlane: "My reason for not going to tell Jones was that I did not want to be assassinated myself. I couldn't give my life for all these men in the court house. I would not sacrifice my own life for that of Jones or any other man."

Defense: "How many murders were attributed to the organization since you became a member of it?"

At this point Gowen objected on the grounds that to answer would be to defeat the ends of justice. He said several murderers were still at large and that when they were arrested would be the time to have them exposed.

Defense Attorney Ryon accused McParlane of being an informer, an "organizer of crime, a setter-up of jobs. While you were investigating the organization, the county was a carnival of crime."

McParlane was now "grinding his teeth" but admitted, "I guess five or six murders were committed since I became a member. I had some knowledge of three murders before their commission and of four or five others attempted. I was three miles away from one, five miles from another and thirty to forty miles from the third."

He admitted learning on July 17 that a man was to be murdered in September. He said he communicated with Franklin shortly after the murders of Sanger and Uren at Raven Run.

McParlane said, "My calculation was that the murder of Sanger was to take place at noon on the day I heard of it. I could do nothing on account of my own safety. I couldn't possibly do more than I did."

The defense asked, "Did you notify the police?"

McParlane replied, "If I did I would be followed all day and if I was seen communicating with an officer I would have been in the same boat as the murdered man. I did not know who was to be murdered. I knew that it was to be a mine boss. I had no acquaintances in Raven Run. I was satisfied in my own mind that the murder was committed the day I was told of it and I had no way of preventing it. I thought I might be watched as I was one of the few who knew of it."

The defense asked, "Did you tell Jack Kehoe, the high constable?"

McParlane said, "No."

The defense continued, "Didn't you ask him for the names of the bosses at Raven Run?"

McParlane said, "No."

The detective denied offering $300.00 to Mike Clark, of Palo Alto, to kill Superintendent Wheeler, who had fired Clark.

He admitted knowing of a plot to kill Forsythia, a mine boss at the Kohinoor Colliery in Shenandoah. He knew Gomer Jones was in danger.

The detective said that Captain Linden was the only man in the region "who was aware of my true character."

McParlane said he was paid $12.00 a week, "and expenses."

He testified that in the spring of 1875 he was told by his friend, Frank McAndrew, that there was a conspiracy to burn down a bridge between Shamokin and Sunbury. He said coal passed over the bridge and this was obviously the reason to destroy it.

The detective testified that he delayed the action by persuading several men that some time was needed to properly organize and execute the plot.

"This gave me time to send word to Superintendent Franklin. I told the men that no good could come of blowing up the bridge. I sent my message by cipher on a telegram.

"I also learned of a plot to burn down the Enterprise Breaker in Sunbury and the Heffenstein Breaker in the same general area."

McParlane swore he secured a pistol from Thomas Hurley after an argument about good pistols, "I got it from Hurley in Shenandoah after charging him with stealing mine from Pottsville. Hurley said to me, 'Here, take this pistol. It is the one that shot Gomer James.' I went to Kehoe to arrange a collection from each Division to make up a present for Hurley. Kehoe said Hurley should get $500.00 instead of the usual one hundred."

At the convention in Tamaqua on August 25, McParlane served as secretary. When the question came about the gift for Hurley, an objection was voiced by Pat Butler.

"It was agreed to investigate the claim of Hurley and I was picked for the committee. Later I reported that Hurley was entitled to the money."

McParlane suggested getting Doyle and Kelly out of jail, and Kehoe said he would do this himself. "My reason for making the suggestion was to see if there was a plot to release them."

When McParlane testified that he would report incidents to his superiors in the Mollies, attorney John Ryon, for the defense, interjected: "You had no superior officers in the organization. You were the head."

While the trial was in progress in Pottsville, a boiler exploded at the Indian Ridge Colliery near Shenandoah. James E. Laughlin was killed. At the inquest it was learned the boiler was *"near worn out"* and not fit to carry the necessary amount of steam for the job. Yet no record was found of any charges of negligence on the part of the company.

———————

Aunt Mamie Zimmermuth looked out over the daisy-embellished mountainside from her parlor window. The pleasing scent of laurel and lilac in bloom reached her nostrils. She smiled at the delightful cries of children on the winding pathways along the banks of Mahanoy Creek.

Tips of tall trees, touching a crescent moon, scattered oblique shadows over sprawling clusters of shrubbery. Soon the laughter of the children at play would fade and stop, with the rising moon serving as the curfew in the mine patch.

Aunt Mamie turned away from the window, her mind on notes piled high earlier by her two young friends. They had gone together to a church strawberry festival. It was the first time Marie attended a Catholic Church program.

Checking the records she noted the detective, James McParlane, was still on the stand, offering testimony. It was May 11, 1876, and the Yost murder trial was still in progress.

McParlane told the court he first learned he was suspected in February of 1876. He testified that men in Shenandoah and Girardville were making bets he would go on the stand as an informer or a detective.

McParlane said that his friend, Frank McAndrew, warned him on several occasions. "McAndrew told me that Mrs. Kehoe told Dan McHughes that McKenna was not to be trusted." How did she know? A conductor on a trolley car talked to her one day in Girardville and McParlane said he believed that this was the first person to question his real identity.

McParlane decided to "face up" to the King of the Mollies. He went to the Kehoe home in Girardville where Kehoe said he had evidence that would prove 'that you are a detective."

Determined to "bluff it out" McParlane called for a convention of all Divisions in the county. "I'll take this fight to the convention floor," he testified. Kehoe not only agreed but asked the detective to address a note to each Body Master.

McParlane said he hoped by this daring move to get all Body Masters together and arrange for their arrests with a dramatic raid on the convention.

It was never held. Kehoe apparently decided to take no chances. He went to McAndrew and was quoted by the detective as saying, "For God's sake, have McKenna shot or he will hang half of Schuylkill County."

At this point in the trial McParlane credited McAndrew with "saving my life" by keeping him posted on the proceedings. "McAndrew said he did not know if I was a detective, but he did not care. He told me to watch a conductor named McDermott on the Shenandoah branch of the trolley line."

McParlane testified that he then went to visit Father D. O. O'Conner in his parish rectory at Mahanoy Plane. "The night before this, McAndrew told me not to go to my boarding room in Cooney's home, but to stay with him. McAndrew told me one man had asked him for a pistol to take a shot at me. His name is Dennis Dowling.

"I went to Pottsville and stayed there overnight. I tired to reach Captain Linden but failed. I didn't know it at the time but the captain had five men shadow me for protection.

"I told Father O'Connor there was a man named James McKenna and I understood this man was representing me as being a detective. The priest not only told me he had heard this but added that he believed that I knew of outrages some time prior to their commission.

"I told him such was not the case; that I could not be a detective. I defended the case of the Irish. I did not know that they committed any outrages at all. There was a great deal more said to their charge than they were guilty of."

"I understood you were a Chicago detective in the employ of the Pinkerton Agency," the priest said, "and that you were paid by this agency and the Pinkertons, in turn, were paid by the coal company for your services."

McParlane testified that the priest said that "it appears like you were implicated in the murder of Jones, or at least Yost. You were seen in the company of Kerrigan immediately after the murder of Yost."

After this conversation with the priest the detective returned to Pottsville and then on to Philadelphia.

McParlane returned for the trial.

Noah Houser took the stand. He and Yost were married to sisters. He was present when Yost died.

"I asked Yost if it was Duffy or Kerrigan who shot him and he said 'No, it wasn't.' I asked him if he was sure and he said, 'Yes, I am sure.' That's all I know."

William Lebo was justice of the peace at the time. He was asked if there was any difficulty between Yost and Duffy.

"Yost and the chief burgess brought Duffy into my office. I heard the case and fined Duffy $5.00 and costs. He conducted himself badly and Yost, to protect himself, had been compelled to use his billy freely. Duffy was so badly beaten that he was laid up for some time."

Lebo testified that "it was an ordinary thing for Kerrigan to get in trouble."

Barney McCarron was the man with Yost at the time of the murder and McCarron said that "the light was not put out when the shots broke out."

May 12, 1876

There was a momentary pause in the Yost murder trail as two men, handcuffed together, were brought into court. They were Charles McAllister and Thomas Munley, both charged with the murder of Thomas Sanger. After some arguments by lawyers, the two men said not guilty to the charge, and this case was continued.

The Yost trial resumed and excitement broke out when James Kerrigan was called to the stand.

The defense protested vigorously on the grounds that Kerrigan was the originator and perpetrator of the murder of Yost and "because he was charged with being one of the principal figures in the murder of John P. Jones." The defense argued that he was incompetent as a witness.

It was overruled.

Kerrigan said, "I didn't see Duffy when he was put in the lockup, but I saw him in Lebo's office and he had marks of violence on him. He showed me a cut on his forehead and said Yost did it.

"I heard Duffy tell Roarty he would give him ten dollars to put Yost out of the road. Duffy said he would do it, or get two other men who would do it. Roarty told me he had McGeghan and Tom Mulhall picked to shot Yost. McGeghan shot him; I saw it."

The defense questioned him, "How far away were you from McGeghan?"

Kerrigan answered, "Sixty or seventy yards."

A pistol was produced and Kerrigan identified it. He said he gave it to a man named Pat McNealis for Roarty. However, McKenna took the pistol out of Kerrigan's hand and cocked it.

"Campbell also gave me a pistol to shoot Jones. I also saw pistols at Alex Campbell's that were brought there by Hugh McGeghan the night before Jones was shot. Campbell gave them to Kelly and Doyle.

"James McKenna was a leading Molly. I exchanged signs with once or twice. I know nothing at all about why I haven't been on trial.

"I did not say to my wife that I shot Yost, but I did tell her that I was with two men from Summit Hill who shot him and she said, 'It is damn good for him, Jim.'

"I did not tell my sister-in-law, Mary Higgins, that I shot Yost."

When cross-examined Kerrigan admitted that he gave the pistol to McNealis after Yost was shot.

Kerrigan replied, "I don't remember whether I told McKenna that now that Yost was out of the way I would like to get some men to kill Jones. I couldn't write so I had to get Jim Carroll to apply to the Shenandoah Division for men to kill Jones. If a man was to be killed, I had to look for the men. That was the rule. I did not tell Jack Kehoe that I tore my pants when I murdered Yost.

"I did go to McKenna to get him to use his influence in getting men for Campbell to kill Jones. I know the coal and iron police told Jones he was in danger. One guard was placed at the Jones home and later two, and they were there for five nights. Since he was guarded by the night the plan was to kill him by day."

May 13

Several witnesses testified that they saw one or more of the five prisoners in or about Tamaqua the day before the murder.

Charles Allen saw Kerrigan at midnight outside the United States Hotel.

Pat Nolan said Kerrigan "came into my saloon on July fifth at about 10:30 P.M. He called me into the back room and asked me if I would lend him a pistol."

George Weldon saw Kerrigan at 1:00 A.M. on July 6 outside the Broadway House in Tamaqua.

Richard Curnow, of Tamaqua, saw Thomas Duffy early in the evening of July 5. He also saw another "large built man," with a coat "about the same color as Mr. Ryon wears, a brown coat."

(Aunt Mamie noted that the records showed that Ryon wore a black coat.)

Edward Shoemaker could not tell why he remembered seeing McGeghan passing through town when he couldn't recall seeing anyone else. (Shoemaker was accepted as a witness although he had once been charged with cruelty to animals and was once convicted of stealing money from Cooney Correll. He had served time.)

William H. Evans, a mine foreman, testified that James Boyle worked on July 6. "He and his buddy, Pat Dawson, loaded six mine cars on a sixty-eight-degree pitch."

Chris Maloney, an operator for Western Union Telegraph at Tamaqua: "I saw Thomas Duffy pass the U.S. Hotel at 5:25 A.M. on July sixth."

May 15 (Monday)

It was established that Duffy ran an engine at the Buckville Colliery on July 6. The outside foreman said Duffy also worked on July 5.

John Kolb testified, "I am freight and ticket agent at Lansford. I have a recollection of selling McGeghan tickets to Tamaqua prior to his arrest."

When cross-examined Kolb said he could not tell how often or what time McGeghan was at the station but he did remember that the tickets were not to Mauch Chunk.

John Churchill testified that he was acquainted with James Kerrigan and almost ran over him while driving a wagon. However, he could not remember the day of the week "and I wouldn't swear about the day of the month."

Attorney Gowen called Father O'Connor to the stand but the priest was not present. Someone spoke out the priest had missed his train.

Here is what Kalbfus said in his address to the jury, "There are only two witnesses introduced upon whose testimony you are to judge the guilt of these prisoners. One is an informer and the other is an accomplice.

"Kerrigan was a Body Master of a respectable organization until he, and others like him, prostituted it. In prison he is fed upon bananas, candy, peanuts and the best. McKenna, or whoever he is, has testified to you concerning the origin of the AOH and has called it the Molly Maguires, and as you understand that name it is enough to convict an innocent man. He spent three or four days on every murder that took place from the time he entered the county until he went away.

"These men are not on trial for having killed Sanger or Uren, or Gomer Jones, or John P. Jones, or any other murdered men he told you about. They are on trial for the murder of Franklin B. Yost.

"Two of the men have not had one single word testified against them."

The defense insisted, "We can prove McKenna's dates are wrong and that he lied under oath, and we shall show you that from the time he came until he went there was a perfect carnival of crime in this county.

"On the night he heard that Jones was to be murdered he went to bed. We shall show you that Kerrigan killed Yost. He and another man-never named-did that devilish deed. Immediately after the killing he went to a party where he said he had killed him.

"The pistol here in court that fired the shot that made a hole in McGeghan's counter is the property of Kerrigan, the murderer and outlaw of this county.

"McKenna was not at the scene of any murder. You will remember this. He planned them and instigated them, but he was not present at any of them."

"We intend to use not only defense witnesses but Commonwealth witnesses to show the prisoners were not at the scene of the murder and therefore could not be guilty."

Father O'Connor was present when called the second time and he said that a man representing himself as James McKenna spent fifteen or twenty minutes in the parish rectory on March 13.

Mrs. Alex Campbell swore that Kerrigan was not in her home on July 6 as he had stated, and the black pistol admitted as evidence "looks like the one he gave me to keep for him on December thirtieth, 1874."

Thomas Trainer, a neighbor of Kerrigan's, said that "Kerrigan turned to me and said: 'Tom, you know Yost made a hellish roar when he was shot.' He must have been at the murder if he heard the roaring."

Pat Duffy testified that Kerrigan was once sent to jail after a fist fight. Duffy swore that Kerrigan said, "When I get out I'll kill Yost the first chance I get."

Pat Dawson, of Summit Hill, swore he saw James Boyle at work on July 6. "I loaded coal from his mine breast. He worked all day. We started at 7:00 A.M. and quit some time between 5:00 and 6:00 P.M. We didn't work less that day than any other day."

Gowen attempted to have the witness contradict this testimony. At one point the attorney turned to the jury and said: "Surely, enough has already been proven to convict every member of the organization to murder in the first degree."

William H. Evans, mine boss, said Boyle was at work on July 6 and loaded six mine cars with Dawson.

Several witnesses testified being with one or more of the five defendants the night before the murder. The defense said that it appeared or seemed to be that if the Commonwealth could prove a man a Mollie he was automatically guilty. The defense also argued that the pistol that shot Yost was owned by Kerrigan.

When Kerrigan said the five prisoners were in the kitchen of Mrs. Catherine O'Donnell's home with him, she swore that she was the sole occupant of the home when Kerrigan was there.

He admitted attending four conventions and was Body Master when Jones was killed and was also Body Master when Yost was killed. He filled this post in the organization although he could not read or write.

When a defense attorney made reference to the new clothes on Kerrigan, he replied, "My own clothes were worn and I couldn't come down from Mauch Chunk in my skin."

When one of the defense attorneys accused Kerrigan of telling Jack Kehoe, "I tore my pants when I murdered Yost," he said with a note of pride, "My clothes were worn out in the service of the Molly Maguires in leading men to commit murder."

Chapter 5

THE TRIALS CONTINUE

Lots were selling in a new coal town called Catawissa Valley and at Girard Manor for one hundred and fifty dollars. They measured 150 by 40 feet with a five per cent discount allowed to cash customers. Others paid five per cent at the time of purchase and monthly payments of $2.85.

The Shenandoah Valley Bank was buying and selling gold, silver and "all kinds of bonds with interest allowed to all depositors."

M. J. Cleary had pure old rye whiskey, up to eight years of age, on sale at "prices lower than the lowest." Train schedules, on double tracks, were announced daily.

Names of residents who had letters "not called for" at the post office were announced in newspapers. The Shamokin Guards sponsored a "hop" in the Douty Hall. "It was a grand success, with one exception. The music was very poor."

Advertisements appeared, during the Molly Trials, for "Mollieism Illustrated," accurate portraits and illustrations of leading criminals. The "Haas Expectorant" was the great remedy for coughs, colds consumption "and all diseases of the throat and lungs. It never fails to cure when properly used. It is the best family medicine for pulmonary disease extant." Footnotes by bank presidents declared the claim was "no humbug."

It wasn't hard to sell newspaper advertisement space or the paper itself, as just about everybody who could read kept up with the daily accounts of the Yost murder trial.

Adam Hartwig, recorder in the county, testified that he saw Roarty on July 5 outside Carroll's café "with four or five other men."

The defense started, "Did you know any of the men with Roarty?"

Hartwig replied, "No."

The defense ended, "That is all."

John W. Kantner, a plumber with a reputation for drinking, a reputation created by people Kantner said couldn't handle it as well as could, saw Kerrigan, McGeghan and Carroll "with a few others" in Carroll's saloon at 11:30 P.M. on July 5. He testified leaving this place and going to one called Rab's Café.

The defense asked, "Why did you go there?"

Kantner said, "It was for personal reasons."

The defense chided him and Kantner blurted, "I'll tell you. I went there looking for a whiskey still. I did not find any."

Attorney Ryon, for the defense said, "I guess there isn't one there or you would have found it."

Andrew Linsay was a flour sack manufacturer but he also repaired sewing machines. He was handed a pistol and he said a screw in the gun came from a sewing machine. "I think I put it there."

Lindsay said that he had seen the prisoners before and one of them had brought the pistol to him for repairs and two others later called for it. He swore he knew James Roarty by sight.

Roarty stood up.

"I think I have seen him before," Lindsay said.

When cross-examined and told the pistol might be the murder weapon, Lindsay couldn't swear the pistol was "ever in my possession. When I first looked at it I got the impression I had seen it before. On second sight I remember there was a rod in that pistol I repaired and this one has only a part of a rod in it."

May 17, 1876

On this day witnesses appeared for the defense.

J. W. Raudenbush, former sheriff of Carbon County, said Carroll's character was "always good." Francis Stocker, the new sheriff, said he had known Carroll since 1840 and knew him as a man of good character. He added that Carroll "helps me build sheds, fences, and hog houses."

Mrs. Kerrigan said her husband had shot Yost. "He left the house with a pistol at dusk on July fifth and returned before dawn the next morning and told me he had shot Yost." She visited with him in jail until she heard he "confessed." She never went again.

On the witness stand she said: "I didn't send him his clothes because he wants innocent men to suffer for his crimes. Why should I go see a man guilty of such a crime as that of Yost's murder? Yes, I lived with him after the crime. If I had disclosed him, he would have shot me. He threatened me and said he would blow out my brains. I treated him as a wife until he turned informer."

Mrs. Kerrigan testified that when her husband got home about four o'clock in the morning "his pants were torn and I mended them while he slept."

The Kerrigans had four children.

May 18, 1876

Dr. James Donahue, of Summit Hill, testified that he was called to visit Mrs. Roarty on the evening prior to the

134

murder. "I asked for someone to go for medicine. Mr. Roarty came with me and it was 9:00 P.M. when he left my office."

Mrs. Madge O'Donnell said Hugh McGeghan was "on the blacklist and could not get a job."

Edward Gillespie said he was on his way home on July 5 and "Kerrigan called over to me and asked me for a revolver. He said he was going to shoot a cop. I assured him I had no gun."

———————

Regional news columns of the day included the following: "Frank McAndrew, who was mentioned by McParlane as having saved his life, has found it necessary to change his quarters and has left town for the present."

In spite of the disreputable character portrayed in news releases after Kerrigan testified against the Mollies, one published observation noted that "Kerrigan is a very large nail in the coffin of the prisoners, though not as much as he ought to be. He has retrieved himself to some extent by turning state's evidence."

"Defeat by the defense means not only the death of five men but of many more, and the total destruction of an order which would poison the atmosphere of hell."

On Friday, May 20, 1876, a summary of the developments against the Mollies was published. It listed twenty members of the AOH arrested for murder, two convicted, five on trial and thirteen yet to be tried.

That night a man acting in a suspicious manner at the Kohinoor Colliery was shot "and probably killed by a night watchman. The man was carried off by confederates." This was never solved.

The next day two men were accused of setting fire to the Turkey Run mine. Over this same weekend it was noted that a member of the jury, Levi Stein, was in ill health.

During the following week Roarty and "Yellow Jack" Donahue were charged with conspiracy to kill William and Jesse Major, brothers, F. W. Langdon, ticket boss at

Audenreid, who was clubbed severely and died three days after the attack.

The cry of "death to all Mollies" resounded from one end of the coal region to the other.

On May 24, Levi Stein, the juror, died and the next juror was discharged.

On June 1, Charles Dress, night watchman at the Kohinoor Colliery, received a "Coffin Notice" that said, "You have ten days time to leave."

On June 2, two hundred men went on strike at the Shoemaker Colliery. The action was prompted by a notice posted at the mine operation: "Workers are expected to start at 6:45 A.M. and quit at 12 noon; start again at 1:00 P.M. and work until 6:00 P.M."

One of the chief protests was about starting work at 6:45 A.M. instead of 7:00 A.M. A company official explained, "This is because on Saturday we shut down at 4:30 P.M. and this is to make up the hour-and-a-half."

Even the newspapers sided to some extent with the miners in this fight. One release noted that "no men follow a more precarious and unsatisfactory mode of life than miners. The men can't be blamed for kicking against working these extra hours." The same release added that the men should have continued to work "and endeavor to gain their ends by pacific measures."

That very day fire broke out in the engine room of the Diamond Shaft. The room was 236 feet underground and twenty-six mules smothered. Machinists were blamed "because sparks dropped from their lamps."

On June 3 it was publicly noted that there were nine "Mollies in the jail at Mauch Chunk and twenty-one in Pottsville."

Two days later McParlane, after working two days mining coal at Indian Ridge, quit and said he was never intended to be a miner. "It took him several days to straighten up."

A dance was organized, ostensibly for the benefit of Frank McAndrew, the Body Master who had returned to

Shenandoah. In reality it was held to raise money for the defense of Kelly, Doyle and Kerrigan. One of the leaders in the movement was McParlane. He bought rounds of drinks and sang "The Mollie Song."

Tom Hurley, who was the "murderer of Gomer James," roomed with McParlane at one time. He was accused of stealing money from a trunk in the room where he found several letters from a "B. Franklin."

A body of men known as the "Coal and Iron Police" was commissioned by the Governor. This made it official.

John Kehoe, the King of the Mollies, had a "letter to the editor" published:

"We are thoroughly aware that lawless acts have been committed. County newspapers report Molly Maguireism is made synonymous with the AOH, a chartered organization recognized by the Commonwealth. It is composed of men who are law-abiding and seek the elevation of members.

"Nothing can be more unjust than to charge the Order with any acts of lawlessness and nothing can be more inconsistent with the wishes of the people than the agitation of this matter by the leading papers of this county."

The letter went on to explain the AOH being chartered in Pennsylvania on May 10, 1871. "Its by-laws provide for a fine of one dollar for intoxication; 50 cents for profanity and $5 for striking a member. Any member convicted of robbery, perjury or any other atrocious offense will be excluded for life."

Kehoe continued to explain that signs and passwords were for the purpose of preventing any imposition and it was no more "a secret society than the Free Masons or Odd Fellows."

June 10, 1876

Father D. I. McDermott, of New Philadelphia, published a statement: "Today there is no such organization as the Molly Maguires in Schuylkill County. There is an Ancient Order of Hibernians."

McParlane testified he joined the AOH, but after becoming a member discovered he had actually joined the Molly Maguires.

A widely read metropolitan journal called "*Irish World*" blamed the coal operations for the lawlessness in the region. It made particular mention of the Reading Coal and Iron Company.

"The Molly Maguires were urged on to deeds of violence by the cruel treatment of tyrannical bosses. Some of them deserved the death that overtook them. It is not our purpose to shield any man, whether capitalist or laborer, from a just accountability.

"Doubtless the Molly Maguires themselves helped to give color to the belief that crimes were committed by them, hoping thus to terrify the capitalists into a more equitable state of mind.

"The whole trouble originated in the greed and rapacity of those soulless corporations. They are the real conspirators against the peace and good order of

Pennsylvania, though a herd of venal newspapers keep screaming to the contrary."

June 14, 1876

News announcement: "The Alexander Campbell murder trial may open on Monday, June 19. Campbell is charged with complicity to kill John P. Jones."

The trial opened on June 22 in the Mauch Chunk Court at Carbon County. The defense argued for a change of venue.

John Kline testified: "I am one of the Minute Men. We were organized by orders of the sheriff. We received our arms from the government and we were to hold ourselves in readiness to answer any call from the sheriff."

The defense: "This proves beyond doubt, that there was undue excitement. A fair trial cannot be granted the prisoner in this court." Attorney Kalbfus asked that the indictment be quashed: "It does not set forth the manner of the death of John P. Jones or the weapon used. The names put into the wheel from which the grand jury was drawn were selected by the jury commissioners before they were sworn."

The request was denied.

The defense moved to quash the array of petit jurors on the grounds that the persons who drew the names from the wheel were not legally authorized to do so.

This was denied.

The jury was secured from thirty-six names on a panel of sixty. The District Attorney opened the case by explaining that "an accessory is one who is not present at the murder, but is one who is connected with it. Campbell hired the men to do the job."

The D. A. attempted to explain Kerrigan's whereabouts by claiming he was "out looking for his goat."

Margaret Griffiths testified that Kerrigan owned no goat.

The defense asked: "Is the Kerrigan of whom you speak the same man who said that he led two men to kill Yost?" The question was not allowed.

During the trial some witnesses saw two men, some three. Some heard two shots, some three and others weren't sure how many they heard.

One witness swore the bullet hit Jones in the right side of the chest and came out near the base of the spine. Another said it hit in the right arm.

William Parkinson saw two men with Kerrigan on Hunter Street on September 3.

Jacob Liebengood said Kerrigan asked him for a match on the wagon road.

Edward Fibish, a painter, said he heard shots and "saw Jones run down a pipeline calling out, 'Oh, oh, oh.'"

The defense questioned him, "At a distance of 500 yards you heard Jones call out, 'Oh, oh, oh?'"

Fibish answered, "Yes, I did."

The defense stated, "Then that is all."

Kerrigan was called as a witness for the Commonwealth.

The defense protested on the grounds he was incompetent and "the miscreant who planned the murder. This man Kerrigan was present at the time Jones was shot down in cold blood. The testimony given at the trial of Doyle was sufficient to hang Kerrigan and he knew it. Now he finds another man who is being tried for being an accessory before the fact and Your Honors are asked by the Commonwealth to admit this man's evidence, that he may go scot-free and that Alex Campbell may hang in his place."

The objections were overruled.

June 26, 1876

Kerrigan testified that there were twenty to twenty-five Body Masters and "most of them kept grog mills." Campbell operated a saloon in Tamaqua.

Kerrigan said that Campbell wanted men from Mount Laffee to murder Jones. "Since Summit Hill men killed Yost the compliment must be returned by getting Tamaqua area men to kill Jones."

He admitted that he was arrested for killing John P. Jones. He testified: "I did not say I took McGeghan and Boyle to where they were to kill Yost. I was there when they did kill him. I piloted them away when it was done and did say it was a clean job."

He blamed the Mollies for stopping his wife from visiting him in jail.

A gun was placed before Kerrigan. He said: "That is the pistol owned by Roarty that shot Yost, and I saw it done, but I couldn't swear that it killed Jones.

"Yes, I did tell McKenna to use his influence to get men, as Campbell wanted them to kill Jones."

He admitted knowing that Tom Mulhall and Hugh McGeghan had been "on the blacklist."

Kerrigan said there was fear that he would squeal. However Doyle came to him and said, "You don't know anything. You can't squeal."

James McParlane took the stand and reviewed his background and work as a detective. He tended bar for Carroll.

The detective said he had known Campbell, Carroll, Roarty and McGeghan since July 15, 1875. He said he recalled a conversation with Campbell about the murder of Yost and learned that McGeghan was the one who murdered Yost.

He said he reported "from day to day to Benjamin Franklin and filed several such reports in a tin box."

"Kehoe told me that it devolved upon me and James Roarty to assist O'Brien, of Mahanoy City, in killing William Thomas. I told him, of course, I would."

He named the place and date concerning the planned murder of William and James Major. He went with the men "but when I got to Mahanoy City I told O'Brien it was too risky and he agreed."

Thomas was shot but recovered.

McParlane: "I arrived at Tamaqua with the men on September second, 1875, and I took them to Carroll's place. Carroll asked me if the men I had with me had come to kill Jones and I said 'yes'."

The defense: "If Captain Linden, or Allan Pinkerton, or Benjamin Franklin, or any other Benjamin allowed the witness to ingratiate himself with the Molly Maguires and, with them, plan crimes that were contemplated and attempted and not prevented, they are accessories before the fact to those crimes that have been committed."

McParlane: "I found out on July 17 that Mr. Jones was to be murdered and I reported the fact to Mr. Franklin on July 19."

After admitting he was with the men in Mahanoy City to kill Thomas, the detective testified: "As people around saw me with these men, there was no chance for me to prevent them from acting, as my own life would have been lost.

"Father O'Connor told me that I was a detective and that I was wrong to come and help put up such jobs. I told the priest there was nothing wrong with the Molly Maguires."

The detective admitted that he offered to furnish the men and a plan to rescue Kelly and Doyle after he heard rumors that they were to be rescued.

Blazing headlines notified an excited public that the "State Is Closing the Lines Around Campbell" on June 20.

William Callahan testified that he was Body Master in the AOH at Mahanoy Plane "and never heard any propositions made for the killing of men." He was not subpoenaed but appeared because "McParlane slurred me. He was at my house in June and told me that something had to be done about Mahanoy City. He said that 'Bully' Bill was a bad man and he wanted him out of the way. He came the second time and said he had accomplished one job and would try another. He then took a drink at my bar."

The howling headlines certainly did not have much connection with the testimony recorded in the news columns.

In the cross-examination Callahan was asked: "Have you heard Father O'Connor denounce the AOH?"

The defense objected but the question was allowed.

Callahan stated, "I never heard Father O'Connor denounce the AOH as Molly Maguires."

Callahan was a member of the AOH for twelve years. He joined it in Ireland and described the AOH as a "peaceful organization, confined to respectable people of Irish nationality and Roman Catholic faith."

He was asked twice if he had anything to do with a plan to burn down Jackson's Patch. He said, "I was never in Jackson's and I never told McParlane anything about such plans." He explained that the phrase "putting a man out of the way" didn't mean murder, but simply sending him off on a railroad car.

Callahan continued, "I told Joseph Murphy that McParlane was going to kill Gomer James. I also told Jack Kehoe that McParlane intended to kill James and he wouldn't believe me."

Charles Kline testified that Doyle bought cartridges "in my store on September second," and on cross-examination admitted that Kelly and Kerrigan were in the store with Doyle at the time. "It was after candle-light when they left," he said.

Daniel Kenney saw Campbell in Tamaqua on September 4. Kenney and several other witnesses testified that Campbell's character was not good.

However, on cross-examination all admitted reaching this conclusion after the murder of Yost. Some of them said they didn't even know Campbell before that.

Wallace Guss, called to the stand by the Commonwealth, said Yost was killed on the night of July 5 and Jones on September 3 and he never heard of Campbell being spoken of as a bad man before Yost was shot.

Guss said, "There was no vigilance committee, but there was one called a safety organization and it was members of this group who told me Campbell was a bad man."

While on the stand the defense had Guss admit he found a two-dollar bill on the person of Kerrigan "with currency wrapped in it."

Daniel Shepp was a brother-in-law of B. K. Yost. He said he knew Campbell "three or four years by reputation. I believe jobs were set up in saloons owned by Molly Maguires." Campbell kept a saloon and was a Molly, therefore guilty.

Campbell worked in the mines for two years and then went into the business of bottling porter.

John Churchill said he "heard" there was a great deal of "nuisance about Campbell, especially on election day." Here he added a rather strange statement, "I do not think I am at all bound to tell all I know."

Bernard Hayes was a coal miner at Mahanoy City. He testified that "McKenna wanted me to join the AOH. McKenna said to me, 'Barney, says he, why don't you be a man and join the Mollies?' I told him I could join the order any time I wanted to join. I asked McKenna or McParlane about matters which pertained to our people in Ireland and he could not answer me. I then put him down as a counterfeit. I knew then he did not belong to our seed or generation. I told McParlane the Catawissa Bridge could not be burned down because there was not much wood about it. I told him I would have no hand in it."

The Commonwealth immediately produced witnesses who had heard Barney Hayes was a politician, "who made speeches, got drunk and it was rumored did not tell the truth."

Kalbfus stood up and said, "The defense rests."

Faces were pressed against court windows. Excitement was high. Voices were loud. There was a general shuffling for advantageous places. This all took place inside the courtroom.

The trial was momentarily forgotten to watch a runaway horse outside. Soon the horse and wagon disappeared around the corner and all returned to their places.

Attorney Allen Craig opened the case to the jury. After complimenting the jurors he said, "You are sworn to acquit this man Campbell if he is not guilty. We do not ask for the conviction of this prisoner unless we can satisfy you beyond a reasonable doubt that he stands guilty of the crime with which he is charged. But on the other hand if we clearly prove that this man is guilty, the duty you owe to God, your country and yourselves will compel you to bring him in guilty of the charge."

He described the killing of Jones.

"The question now looms up before you as to who are the perpetrators of the cold-blooded and fiendish murder. Now, gentlemen of the jury, we allege on the part of the Commonwealth that the men who killed John P. Jones were Michael Doyle and Edward Kelly. We shall prove to you that the men who committed that murder were procured by this prisoner at the bar, and as the law terms him, he is an accessory before the fact. The court will tell you that it is not necessary for a man to be present at the murder to be a murderer, and we say that although he was not present at the killing of Jones, he is even more guilty than Doyle or Kelly, for he planned and abetted the deed."

Attorney Craig accused Campbell of securing the weapons for the murder and that Doyle and Kelly were instruments in his hands. After a brief review of testimony offered by Commonwealth witnesses he continued, "We have revealed the secrets of the Molly Maguires and raised the cover from the crimes which have been committed. This organization of bandits has the power of murdering, plundering and destroying. It can be traced back to a foreign shore. It is an unnatural plant in this country, and I hope to God it may be uprooted all over the land by courts and jurie. An organization of this kind has no grounds to be among civilized people."

He went on to condemn the organization and all its members and admitted that Kerrigan "is no saint." He said, "Kerrigan is as guilty as Kelly or Doyle, but not as guilty as Campbell."

The lawyer then reviewed the detective work of McParlane. He said, "His object was to detect crime and he had to play a double part; he had to be a *bona fide* Molly Maguire and a detective at the same time. You know this man as McKenna and you know he was appointed with two men to kill Jones and you know how he frustrated the attempt."

He asked the jurors, "Do you believe McParlane? Do you believe he would come on the stand and perjure himself in order to punish Campbell? It is because Campbell caused the life of Jones to be taken."

Craig then refuted all testimony offered by the defense. He said much of it was conflicting, much of it lies and much of it submitted by known drunks.

Craig spoke for three and one-half hours. When he finished court was adjourned and reconvened for an afternoon session.

Attorney Kalbfus said to the jury, "The Commonwealth wants Alex Campbell hung, not because he killed John P. Jones, but because there are five thousand Molly Maguires in Schuylkill County. When it comes to sifting the evidence you will find Campbell guiltless.

"I look into the books for the admissibility of James Kerrigan's evidence, under the head of infamy. Upon his authority this man is to die and his wife made a widow. Kerrigan is the confessed accomplice of the killing of Yost;

he is the captain of the men who killed Jones. He has no soul; he is a wreck of total depravity.'

"He killed Jones and now wants to kill Campbell. Gentlemen of the jury, do you mean to say that Kerrigan, who has already killed men, would hesitate a moment to go upon that witness stand and swear falsely to save his own life?

"In all the witnesses we have placed upon the stand not one was a Molly Maguire. Ah yes, Callahan. He is an honest man who came here without a subpoena to vindicate himself from what McParlane said about him, and the other side says that he cannot be believed because he is a Molly Maguire. You have heard of one McAndrew, who was also a Molly Maguire, but he said to McParlane, 'I will save your life' and he did."

He refuted testimony by Commonwealth witnesses and urged jurors to believe defense witnesses who took the stand in spite of great pressures.

Kalbfus then turned his attention to McParlane. "Who is this man McParlane? What nerved Brutus to slay Caesar?

He loved him. Why did Booth kill Lincoln? The one answer will do for both questions and that is – ambition."

Kalbfus began to raise his voice dramatically, "Yes, it was ambition that threw Satan over the walls of heaven. I repeat it; who is McParlane?

"He is a teamster, a half-made chemist and a whiskey dealer. He said he killed a man in Buffalo. You heard him say so. He said he was a counterfeiter and was living on counterfeit gains. Under oath he told these things and said he lied. He told Campbell that he had shot a man in Tamaqua. He is the man who incited the burning of the Catawissa Bridge, as testified to by a witness who has not been contradicted. He is the hireling of the Reading Railroad Company. The AOH was an honorable organization until McParlane and Kerrigan disgraced it.

"Who is McParlane? He is the man who wrote to Franklin and told him Gomer James and John P. Jones were to be killed. He did it after the murders were committed. Blast him! Only four miles from the killing of Jones and he would not save his life.

"If they would not accuse me on the other side of being a blackguard I would call him a liar. Coward? He abetted, he planned, he connived the killing of John P. Jones, and you know it.

"He was the man who fixed the rewards for the killing that was done and he was the brains of the society. I say that the only evidence against Alex Campbell is McParlane's, and you are to disbelieve it utterly, if the evidence of the defense contradicts it."

Kalbfus spoke for two and one-half hours.

Kalbfus was followed by Attorney Fox, an associate. He also directed abuse upon McParlane.

"The detectives or informers of Ireland are nothing less than the heresy of English courts. I say that a man who enters a conspiracy and encourages men to commit crime is just as guilty as those who commit the crime. A man who employs a systematic mode of lying in order to gain a desired end is a detestable man.

"It may be necessary in human society that men should enter the bands of criminals to detect crime. But that man's motive should be good alone, and he should not be a conspirer in or an encourager of crime. Now take McParlane upon his own story; he encouraged and promulgated the murder of Jones.

"McParlane is the man who made Mrs. Jones a widow."

He called the detective an informer "upon men with whom he was associated. In McParlane we have a man who not only says he entered the society for the purpose of detecting crime, but when they faltered in an outrageous attempt, he simulated and encouraged these acts."

He accused McParlane of being an accessory before the fact in murder, "Where is the principle in that if a man informs the police of a murder and afterwards takes part in the affair, that he is not part of the murder? There is no such thing in the world."

The Honorable F. W. Hughes addressed the court next, against the prisoner. He asked Irishmen to root out the cancer of Molly Maguireism.

"Gentlemen of the jury," he said proudly, "I am an informer. I have prosecuted Dutch, Welsh, Irish and other nationalities. Without exception this is the most important murder trial ever held in America."

Attorney Hughes continued: "I will try and lead you to the right conclusions, although I may be somewhat partisan or biased in my opinion, and for this reason I would ask you not to be hasty in your verdict."

He explained that Campbell was not charged with the hiring of Doyle and Kelly for the purpose of killing Jones, but he was directly indicted for the murder of Jones. "Under the indictment Campbell is either guilty of murder in the first degree, or not at all."

He described the murder of Jones and reviewed the testimony. He said the evidence showed that Doyle and Kelly were Molly Maguires. He claimed they were selected for the murder because they were members of the organization. "It was the Molly Maguires organization that selected them. The man with whom they stayed was an accomplice. This is the life of the case."

He pointed to the black pistol and said it was the weapon that "killed Yost and Jones and God only knows how many more." He agreed that Kerrigan was "an infamous man and an accomplice, but if his testimony is corroborated you must believe it to be true." He argued eighteen points in which he claimed Kerrigan's testimony was corroborated by other witnesses. He further argued that defense witnesses had committed perjury.

Hughes said, "Kerrigan is a Molly Maguire. He is the murderer of Policeman Yost. But he was led into crime by this man, Alex Campbell, who is his godfather in regard to initiation into the Molly Maguires. I say to you, gentlemen, that Kerrigan is testifying with a rope around his neck in expectation of death and not on account of a pardon."

The Commonwealth attorney then turned his attention to James McParlane, defending his actions and praising his work as a detective. He made a point of conventions being held for the purpose of offering rewards for crime. "and placing the crowns of honor upon successful murderers."

He turned his attention to the Molly Maguires, "We must uproot and destroy this organization. If we are not successful God is not on our side. The other side asked why did not McParlane save the life of Jones. We say his object was not to prevent the killing of any particular man, but to entirely break up the Molly Maguires."

He described McParlane as a man of intelligence and noble qualities; "Now he stands before you as an administrator of justice, a man who has reduced himself to privations that not a man in that jury box would suffer."

He concluded by urging the jurors to "do your duty earnestly and conscientiously."

After this, Judge Dreher charged the jury. He described murder "at common law" and malice aforethought and other points of law in his instructions.

He said, "If the evidence satisfies you beyond a reasonable doubt that Alex Campbell was an accessory before the fact, or an accomplice in the killing of Jones, then you must bring him in as guilty according to the manner and form indicted. If the evidence shows you that the prisoner at the bar hired Doyle and Kelly to kill Jones, then Campbell is just as guilty as if he was present at the killing and took part in it."

Judge Dreher explained that "the rule of the law is that a man may presume that he is not guilty until the Commonwealth proves to the jury, beyond the possibility of a doubt, that he is guilty, and if there is a doubt in your minds as to the guilt of Alex Campbell, a reasonable doubt, a doubt which springs alone out of the evidence, you must give him the benefit of that doubt.

"But if there is nothing in the evidence which causes you to hesitate, then you are to act according to the testimony. The creditability of the witnesses you alone are to determine. When there are contradictions in the testimony of the witnesses, the first duty of the jury is to reconcile the discrepancies until they find that the witnesses have willfully and premeditatedly committed perjury. Human minds are differently constituted, and very frequently discrepancies in the testimony of witnesses may be reconciled, because facts have passed differently under their observation."

The Judge said, "James Kerrigan is an acknowledged accomplice in the murder of Jones. He is therefore an infamous witness and we charge you not to convict the prisoner upon the uncorroborated evidence of this man."

He informed the jurors that the Government had a right to employ the services of a detective; "so McParlane was not an accessory before the fact." He described McParlane as a man of good character and therefore "not an infamous witness and his evidence should be treated by you with as much weight as that of other witnesses.

"However, if the jurors believe that McParlane entered into a conspiracy to kill Jones, or counseled others to do it, then you should not convict on his testimony alone."

Judge Dreher continued his charge, "If you find the defendant guilty, you must say whether he is guilty of murder in the first degree or in the second degree. You can now retire, and as soon as you have made up a verdict the court house bell will toll."

It was eight-fifteen that evening when the bell sounded, in short, quick peals.

The jury filed into a court room filled to the walls. After some pushing and pulling in the aisles, it became suddenly quiet.

Judge Dreher asked, "Have you reached a verdict?"

William F. Roberts, the foreman of the jury said, "Yes, your honor."

Judge Dreher asked, "What is it?"

Roberts replied, "Guilty of murder in the first degree."

Chapter 6

MUNLEY AND McALLISTER

Pat Mulrooney found Aunt Mamie asleep in her favorite chair. Cuffed by her hand and downward on the table, her face was hidden by her ruffled abundance of gray hair.

The notes on the Alex Campbell murder case were compiled and placed neatly in one pile at the far edge of the table. Pat pulled up another chair and began reading the notes.

He was lost to all about him and didn't hear her voice until she repeated, "Where's Marie?"

He looked up. Aunt Mamie had not lifted her head.

"She left me."

Aunt Mamie lifted her head.

"Why?"

"My mother called her a German harlot at the strawberry festival."

"So you intend to lose yourself in the Molly Maguires?"

"Yes, I guess so. By the way, Aunt Mamie, was Alex Campbell guilty?"

"Well, his lawyers appealed. Here, I have more notes on the case."

* * * * *

It was Attorney Kalbfus who asked that the prisoner be granted a new trial and presented eight reasons for the action.

The list:

1. The verdict is against the law and the evidence.
2. The verdict is against the weight of the evidence.
3. The court erred in admitting evidence tending to show that the defendant was an accessory before the fact to the killing of John P. Jones, by a pistol shot fired by Michael J. Doyle or Edward Kelly in the absence of the defendant.

4. The evidence showed that James Kerrigan was an accomplice in the murder and as he was not corroborated in material points the jury ought to have acquitted the defendant.

5. James Kerrigan went upon the witness stand as an infamous witness, tainted with suspicion, and as he was contradicted in material points by the testimony of credible witnesses, the jury ought to have acquitted the defendant.

6. The evidence of James McParlane showed that he was an accessory before the fact, and he was not corroborated in material points, the jury ought to have acquitted the defendant.

7. The testimony of McParlane having been contradicted in material points by the evidence of credible witnesses, the jury ought to have acquitted the defendant.

8. The court erred in the exercise of their discretion in permitting James Kerrigan to testify as a witness.

Argument on the appeal was postponed until July 24. Although this date was three weeks away, one newspaper observed:

"There is not any likelihood of the petition for a new trial being granted."

(That preconceived judgment was certainly presumptuous, it was noted by Pat Mulrooney.)

Alex Campbell was brought into court on July 24, and after arguments on the appeal were heard the Judge reserved or delayed his decision until August 28.

The lawyers for Campbell insisted that the testimony of both McParlane and Kerrigan should not have been allowed. Attorney Fox also contended there was "too much undue excitement" and adverse public sentiment for a fair trial.

He related meeting a clergyman the previous day and repeated the following conversation:

The clergyman asked, "You have been defending one of the Molly Maguires at Mauch Chunk lately?"

Fox replied, "I defended a man who was charged with being one and I am going there tomorrow to argue the motion for a new trial."

The clergyman continued, "I hope they will hang him before you get there."

General Albright supported the indictment against Campbell and he was followed by Attorney Hughes who agreed with Mr. Fox that the Judge made two mistakes in his charge to the jury. However Hughes declared the "errors were in favor of the prisoner."

In reserving his decision until the next term of court, the Judge pointed out that the arguments were lengthy and would take some time to study.

One news release at this point turned its attention to Campbell and noted he was being remanded to jail. However "before he was taken out all the women kissed him and to one of them who said something to him in pity, he remarked, 'Never mind, it will be all right'."

Promptly at two o'clock on the afternoon of Monday, August 28, 1876, the courthouse doors at Mauch Chunk yielded to a key in the latch and curious spectators soon filled the courtroom. Judge Dreher and Associate Judges Houston and Wentz occupied the bench.

Campbell was described as being composed, a characteristic noted throughout his trial and confinement.

Judge Dreher, without delay, announced, "This is the day appointed for the disposition of the motion on a rule for a new trial in the case of Alexander Campbell." He said counsel for the defense filed eight reasons – later adding five – for a new trial. The Judge gave his opinion in detail for not entertaining any of them and then concluded: "The rule for a new trial is discharged."

He then called Campbell to "come before the court." The handsome prisoner stood as at attention, facing the bench without any visible expression.

The Judge said, "This is most unpleasant, this duty I must perform. I deeply commiserate with you and your relatives and wife in the unfortunate position in which you are placed. But I also remember the tears of the bereaved wife and orphans of John P. Jones. Yet no feeling for either the dead or living must swerve us from the path of duty. The law of God and man must be observed. I refrain from further comment and ask you, Alexander Campbell, have you naught to say, why the judgment of the law of Pennsylvania should not be pronounced?"

Campbell replied, "Only this, Judge; I am innocent of this crime before God, and I am willing to suffer for the guilty. There is too much prejudice against me in the courts for me to have a fair trial."

Judge Dreher said, "You are yet a young man. Up to the time when you were arrested for this crime you were associated in toil with the men whom a jury of the citizens of this county have said are guilty. You abetted and advised them in the homicide and have been found guilty as a principal in the crime.

"To me this is a most fearful task, but I have nothing more to say, only this; that the sentence of the court is that you, Alex Campbell, be taken from hence to the county jail, and from there to the place of execution, and that you there be hanged by the neck until you are dead, and may God in His infinite goodness, have mercy upon your soul."

On his way back to his cell Campbell issued a statement to a newsman, "Several fellows went on the stand to blacken my character and swore I was all the time fighting with mining bosses, when the only boss I ever worked with swore that I was peaceful and quiet."

Mulrooney looked up, Aunt Mamie was slumped back now in a rocking chair, hands loosely clasped, thumbs twirling first one way and then the other. She was wide awake and looking intently at the young man. Pat's eyes, as they met Aunt Mamie's, were filled with uncertainty and perplexity.

He asked bluntly, "What's a harlot?"

Thomas Sanger was on his way to the large colliery operation at Raven Run where he was engaged as inside mine foreman for the past three years.

It was shortly before seven o'clock on the morning of September 1, 1875. Although unaccompanied, the thirty-three year old mine executive was not alone. Two men walked together about twenty yards behind Sanger. They were William Uren and Richard Andrews, two employees of the same mine. Uren lived as a boarder with the Sanger family.

Suddenly five men appeared in the roadway ahead. One of the five strangers walked ahead of the other four. He stopped only a few yards in front of Sanger and fired a shot from one of two revolvers he carried.

Sanger was hit. He turned and ran toward the nearby Wheevill home. He crossed the front entrance and staggered toward the rear door. The stranger with the two pistols followed and fired again. Sanger fell. The gunman turned him over with his foot and again pulled the trigger.

After Sanger was first hit, other shots were fired and one of them struck Uren.

Holding his right side with his left hand, Uren turned to Andrews and said, "I'm shot, Dick."

Andrews said, "Where, Bill?"

Uren replied, "In my side."

Andrews looked sharply at Uren and, apparently unaware of the seriousness of the wound, said, "You are all right. Let's go look for Tom."

Sanger managed to get on his feet. After firing point blank at the mine boss, the stranger had fled.

Mrs. Robert Wheevill was attracted by the sound of the shots. She ran to the door and Sanger fell inside. She reached for him and fell to the floor with Sanger.

He whispered, "I'm shot." A few minutes later Sanger died in the woman's arms.

Sanger was born in Cornwall, England. His father was a Methodist Minister. His survivors included a wife, six children and four sisters.

William Uren died in the Sanger home on the afternoon of the day he was shot. He was carried from the roadway to the home by fellow mine workers.

Also a native of Cornwall, England, he was only twenty-two years of age when he was mortally shot. He was one of nine children.

There was a great deal of confusion at Raven Run that morning. Andrews (some historians record the name as Anderson) the man with Uren when the shooting took place, dashed for the breaker and then turned to the engine house. Robert Heaton was in the engine room tending to a fire at the time. When he heard the shooting, he ran to the mule stable, got out a horse and went after the gunmen.

He stopped at the Wheevill home where he secured a pistol and fired shots into nearby woods. He got the gun from Robert Wheevill, who saw the strangers and heard the shots and ran back into his home.

Several men on their way to work ran for cover when they heard the shooting. Robert Green shielded himself behind a stout tree. John Hester crawled under a mule stable. John Purcell hid behind the engine house. Luke McHale watched quietly from a safe distance and later in court testified seeing the five men.

William McLaughlin talked with the strangers before the shooting and said they were looking for jobs. William Curran passed the time of day with one stranger near the engine house. John Bolton saw a man on the porch of the Williams home during the shooting.

Two of the men who ran for cover were first confronted by the gunmen. Hester was only a few feet from the man who appeared to be the leader and the man said gruffly, "Clear out."

Purcell was accosted by one of the other men in a similar manner and was ordered curtly to "get out of the way."

In spite of all the witnesses at the colliery that morning only three would swear that one of the five strangers was Thomas Munley and only one of these witnesses was a man. Some of the shots fired by Heaton were answered by shots from the thick underbrush that lined the colliery road. Volunteers joined colliery officials and formed a search party. The woods were searched throughout the morning with the men armed with guns and clubs.

Six months later Thomas Munley and Charles McAllister were arrested for the double murder.

Pat Mulrooney finished reading the description of the double murder. He turned to Aunt Mamie."

"This is your version?"

"No, Marie was here this afternoon."

"Oh, she was, was she?" He paused. It was obvious to Aunt Mamie that Pat was pleased Marie had returned.

"This description seems one-sided," he said. "She makes the Irish look like the devil himself. Just because she's mad at my mother doesn't mean she should take it out on all the Irish."

Aunt Mamie said, "Let us see if she is prejudiced. Let's pick up the highlights of the court case."

Pat agreed.

The murder trial opened on June 26, 1876, in Pottsville. Thomas Munley and Charles McAllister were brought into court together, escorted by the sheriff and four officers. In addition to this precaution, the prisoners were chained.

The defense lineup included attorneys L'Velle, Bartholomew and Ryon. The prosecution chose the district attorney, Guy Farquhar and Franklin B. Gowen.

After a great deal of "conscientious scruples" in choosing jurors the first was finally accepted. He was John T. Klause, of Orwigsburg. The twelfth was picked three days later.

The fifth juror was Tom Fennell. He said, "I have heard and read about this case. I have formed an opinion; it is a strong opinion. But I would be governed by the evidence."

"I mean by bias, that I cannot divest myself of my opinion against a certain organization. I feel that I cannot divest myself of a large amount of prejudice."

Another said, "My prejudice is such against the class of men to which the prisoner belongs that I would not like to sit on the jury. My reason for not liking to serve is the fear of my prejudice influencing me."

The twelve jurors were John T. Clouse, J. W. White, John Springer, Ben Gulding, Tom Fennell, Emanual Garis,

Solomon Fiddler, Daniel Zerbe, Frederick Alvord, Charles Brenneman, Jefferson Dull and Daniel Donne.

The prosecution opened by delving into "the way Mollies manage their business." The constitution was considered a blind to cover crime. The signs, the passwords and "goods" were reviewed, all originating with the Board of Erin.

Dr. A. B. Sherman, Girardville, testified that Sanger was shot in the right forearm and right groin that produced a fatal hemorrhage. Uren was also shot in the right groin, the doctor said, "almost the same as Sanger."

Some witnesses saw two strangers at the colliery that morning, others saw three, a few saw four and still others saw five.

John Arnold saw five men on the mountain on his way to work from Girardville, but admitted he saw miners stand around every morning. He did not hear a man shout "clear out."

William (Anderson) Andrews admitted that a man in a slouch hat asked if any laborers were wanted "and I said no." He said he was near the engine house when he saw a man "run up the road with a pistol in each hand."

Under cross examination Anderson said he could not identify the man he saw and added that he saw no shooting between this stranger and Heaton. He said, "I couldn't tell if he was the same man who spoke with me earlier, but he was about the same height."

Robert Green, of Girardville, said he walked to work "up through Wildcat and I saw two men on a fence and soon after two more sat with them. They came from the colliery stable. I afterward saw one man go up the road toward where Sanger lived. I heard a shot and saw Sanger run back toward his home. I looked at people scattering as the five men were firing in all directions. One came toward me and shouted twice to clear out and Purcell, behind me, called out, 'My God, what will we do?' and I saw another of the strangers walk toward me and I thought it time to leave."

Green headed for the stables where he joined others he named. When questioned by the defense, Green said the stranger was about five feet, seven inches tall, "about like me." Green was asked to stand and he was over six feet tall. He explained that "I'm higher in my boots."

He said that "the man nearest me on the fence had devilish-looking eyes" and when asked what he meant by this, Green replied, "I have neither Webster or Walker with me, but I will define devilish-looking as being wicked."

Here was Green's enigmatic reply to Gown, "If Munley was there I saw him and if he wasn't there I didn't see him, but to the best of my judgment I didn't see him, until I saw him in prison."

When Richard Anderson testified that he walked with Uren to work that morning he said, "I saw the man's face. He was stooped forward; his complexion was light and he wore a small moustache. I saw the man shoot Sanger. He was shooting a revolver from each hand."

Thomas Munley was asked to stand up.

Anderson said, "That's not the man that I can recognize at all."

Mrs. Jeanette Williams, when she heard the shots, turned to a window in her parlor and saw a man go by. She pointed to Munley.

"That looks like the man."

Both Mr. and Mrs. Robert Wheevill testified. When Wheevill heard the shooting he ran from the colliery to his home to get a gun and it was this weapon that was taken by Heaton who chased the gunmen. On cross-examination Wheevill said two or three shots were fired at Sanger before he fell and two or three more after he fell.

"I never saw the man who shot him up to that time. I do not know Munley. I don't see the man here."

Robert Heaton, however, said he was sure that Munley was one of the four men he saw that morning. Sanger was still alive when Heaton got the gun and Heaton quoted Sanger as saying, "Go for them, Rob."

When Gowen called James McParlane to testify the defense objected on the grounds of "professional ethics."

Gowen said, "No instructions in professional ethics are needed or would be accepted from the defense. I intend to prove that there is an organization in the region whose purpose is to murder and to further prove the prisoner is a member."

McParlane, the secret agent, took the stand. He reviewed his background and experience in the region from the time of his arrival at Port Clinton in October of 1873.

He traveled a great deal throughout the southern anthracite district, going from community to community, and from café to café, "to become known."

The question of his religion came up.

"I am a Catholic," he said. "The principles of my church do not allow lying. I communed with the church on one occasion while in the region. I did confess to Father Cooper in Pottsville in January 1874, that I was flying under false colors.

"After I joined the AOH I did not go to confession. I went to church on Sundays but that was all. However, I at no time abandoned my church or even my religion. I did abandon a portion of my duties and I felt justified in doing this. I did take the obligation of keeping the secrets of the Order. I was not morally bound to keep secrets for an organization that I intended to break up. Yes, I did resort to deception, too numerous to mention, to gain the confidence of these people."

With regard to the murder of Sanger and Uren, the detective said he met Doyle in Lawlor's Café on the day of the murder. He quoted Doyle as saying "all is right." He quoted James O'Donnell as saying they "had done a clean job but they shot two as the second came in their way." McParlane declared that O'Donnell said he was first to shoot Sanger and that Munley got between him and Sanger and also fired shots. Others stood by shooting to intimidate the crowd," McParlane said.

The detective said he slept with Doyle the night before the double murder. "I had heard that morning that a boss was to be shot at Raven Run. Doyle told me he had borrowed a pistol to shoot a boss and he asked me for my coat to prevent detection. I gave him my coat. I didn't dissuade him from going and now I would like to give my reasons."

Attorney Ryon said, "I don't want your reasons."

Answering another question the detective said Munley was a member of the Shenandoah division and lived in Gilberton; Doyle belonged to the Big Mine Run division "and the other three were members of the Turkey Run division."

As secretary in Shenandoah, the secret agent said he was authorized to "give a man a card or the goods while the Body Master was away." He said he knew of no written records of any crime in any division.

He said it was Doyle and James O'Donnell who informed him that Sanger was to be murdered. He had learned this about noon on August 31, the day before the crimes were committed.

The Fourth of July was a young holiday in the nation at the time. On the eve of the holiday the Judge announced that court would adjourn until July 5.

A member of the jury stood up and asked Gowen for permission to fish in the Tumbling Run Dam, a resort owned by the coal company.

Mr. Gowen addressed the court. "As counsel in this case I cannot confer any favors upon the Jury. I had ordered no one to fish in the dam until the black bass are placed there. I will now revoke the order for the Fourth, and allow everyone to fish.

Although Munley and McAllister had entered the courtroom together at the start of the trial, the defense had decided to have them tried separately, and Munley was the first defendant.

Attorney L'Velle opened for the defense. After giving some background on Munley the lawyer said, "Mr. McParlane tells you he came into this county to detect crime. He certainly did not come here to prevent it." He then said the defense would prove that Thomas Munley was not at Raven Run when the murders took place.

Michael Munley, brother of the prisoner, said that at ten minutes to seven that morning he saw the prisoner on his porch. He added that his father was also there at that time.

Luke McHale, of Mahanoy Plane, said he saw the strangers and heard the shooting while he was on his way to work and "I know Tom Munley well and he was not one of them."

William McLaughlin testified that he talked with five men and one of them asked him "to take me to the boss for a job." Munley was not one of the men, he added.

William Curran said he worked at Raven Run and was near the mule stable when he saw four men. "I've known Tom Munley four or five years. I did not see him there that day and I think I would have recognized him if he was there."

Curran said he also knew Mike Boyle, Charles McAllister and the two O'Donnell brothers and "none of them were there."

John Bolton, a resident of Raven Run, said he saw the man on Mrs. Williams' porch and "it was not Munley or anything like Munley."

Michael Mack, who lived the length of three football fields west of the colliery, saw and met a stranger at 6:40 A. M. on his way to work. He later saw two others and finally two more joining the first two along the colliery fence. He said, "I saw five men but I didn't see all of their faces, but I know Munley wasn't there."

On cross-examination Mack said he was never in the AOH and knew nothing about it. He was twenty-nine years old and had worked at Raven Run for nine years.

John Donnelly had worked there ten years. "I met a man along the colliery road," he testified. "I bid him good morning, but I did not know the man. As I passed him I saw four others in clean clothes. Munley was not the man I saw first on the road and I could not say that he was one of the five."

When asked why he didn't report the strangers to the boss, Donnelly said there were men "around the slope every morning looking for jobs."

Mrs. Bridget Hylan, who later moved from Raven Run to Jackson's Mine Patch, said she went to the Munley home on the morning of September 1 for a dress pattern "and Munley was there with his wife and children."

Mrs. Margaret Blackwell lived a few doors from the Wheevill home. She heard shots and ran out on her porch and back in again "for fear I would be shot myself." She saw Sanger lean on a fence but saw no one else. Sanger saw her and said, "If you have a pistol, give it to me." She replied, "No, Tom, we haven't any firearms in the house."

Mrs. Blackwell then said she saw a man "I thought at first was Heaton, but I know it was not that man" and she pointed to Munley in the courtroom. She testified that she got the impression Heaton and Sanger were fighting: "I thought at the time that something had come between them."

John Hester saw a stranger while he was on his way to work that morning. He saw a man fire at Sanger, "I was about six yards away. I never knowed Munley. That is not the man I saw that day." He too, pointed at Munley.

Hester continued, "Another man stepped up to me and put a revolver against my breast. He said nothing, I turned and ran to one of the stables."

Pat Holloren was harnessing a mule when he heard shooting. "I saw Mr. Heaton shooting but I couldn't tell at what."

John Purcell saw a stranger "go up to Tom Sanger as if to ask him for a job. This man had been sitting on a stump. The man fired a shot at Sanger and Sanger turned and ran. Then the man fired a second shot and a third man pointed a revolver at me and told me to clear out. I ran toward the stable."

Purcell stood up in the witness box and pointed to Munley. "That is not the man who shot at Sanger and he isn't the man who put the pistol to me."

Ben Mowery met a stranger and saw three men on a fence. Patrick Tobin saw only two men and met a third "who appeared to be taller than Munley."

Edward Monaghan was a colorful witness. He created some excitement on the stand. He had been a constable in Shenandoah for seven years and testified that he arrested James McKenna in 1874 on a charge of assault and battery. The private detective had beaten a peddler and stole his watch, according to Monaghan.

The witness said McKenna knew of a plot to kill Thomas B. Fielders, reporter for the *Shenandoah Herald*. "I told Fielders his life wasn't worth a cent. McKenna sang to attract attention during a ball in Shenandoah while others were to take care of the reporter, but I interfered and got him out of there."

Monaghan made little of McKenna when he testified that the detective "pulled a gun on James L'Velle in Cleary's bar in Shenandoah and L'Velle took the gun from him and threw the detective out into the street."

On cross-examination Monaghan admitted that McKenna was discharged by the burgess and the peddler was fined.

John Burns was sitting outside his front door on the morning of the murders. He said he saw a small man go after Sanger and saw another "taller man running near the colliery stable."

Burns said he never saw these men before "but I know Thomas Munley and I don't think he was one of the men. I saw Robert Heaton and the man who exchanged shots with him and that man was not Munley."

John O'Donnell was at home that day and saw a man follow Sanger and "in my opinion it wasn't Munley."

Edward Purcell saw Sanger run and stagger and fall. "I never before saw the man who shot him and I didn't know Munley, but he was not the man who shot at Heaton or Sanger."

Patrick Sweeney had worked at raven Run for five years and was at the powder house when he heard a shot. "I saw a man in dark clothes and cap shooting at Mr. Heaton. I know Thomas Munley in the old country and in this country and it was not Munley at Raven Run that day."

Several other witnesses offered similar testimony and a few saw "pigeons fly" over the colliery that morning.

Melinda Bickleman was sixteen years old. She lived with Mrs. Wheevill and heard shooting and saw a man "running up the road and another after him. I saw the prisoner fire at Mr. Heaton but did not see Sanger shot."

Mary Munley, the prisoner's sister, said she saw her brother at seven o'clock that morning at his home. She lived next door, she said.

Attorney Bartholomew told the members of the jury that "you must be satisfied beyond a reasonable doubt of the actual presence of the prisoner at the scene of the murders." He added that the testimony of a professional detective or informer should be weighed by the jury with great caution.

"If the jury believes that McParlane encouraged or advised the crime with which the prisoner stands indicted, he is an accomplice, and unless his evidence is corroborated in its material parts by the evidence of other witnesses, the jury cannot convict upon his evidence."

Attorney Kaercher not only condemned Munley, but he condemned the entire organization as being "unfit for this earth."

He reviewed the testimony offered during the trial, refuting all that was said for the defense. He said, "There is no better defense in the world than a true alibi, but when you set up a false alibi and attempt to bolster it with perjury it becomes strong evidence against the prisoner."

He called on the jury to disregard and disbelieve the testimony of a dozen witnesses who disagreed with the testimony of Commonwealth witnesses. His words give evidence of a growing emotion, "A man cannot be in two places at one time. The evidence of one positive witness is worth more than a hundred of the kind that testified in favor of Munley. All these men are members of a bloody organization."

Attorney L'Velle spoke up for the defense. "In spite of the eulogy upon the Irish race and its church, how does it come that not one of that race sits in the jury box? No one ever has in any case of this kind."

Talking directly to the jurors he continued, "Who wouldn't attempt to save the life of a man who was going to be murdered? Let us go to Tamaqua where McKenna took two men to kill Jones, and while he could have saved that poor man's life, what did he do? He sat down quietly and did nothing.

"Why, since the murder of Charles O'Donnell and Mrs. McAllister in December, should no arrests have been made?"

"You heard Mr. Heaton swear he recognized Munley at a distance of fifty yards. You heard Patrick Coyle swear that McKenna's actions in Mahanoy City during the parade of miners in the summer of 1875,was to keep men in line and keep them in proper order and lead them to murder. We don't have a cemetery to bury the men McKenna was to murder."

The Honorable Mr. Bartholomew reviewed the history of the AOH and considered it an honorable organization outside the anthracite region. "But here they are responsible for crimes that make humanity shudder. Here we have a tale of blood and horror that pales the massacre of Custer and his noble band."

He called the crimes atrocious and "hard to believe that men, without any knowledge of or animosity against a man, will walk out into the broad light of day and take the life of a stranger."

Franklin B. Gowen spoke for almost three hours. He based much of his appeal to the jury on the testimony from Robert Heaton, Mrs. Jeanette Williams and Melinda Bickleman, the three witnesses who identified Munley. He called the testimony offered by members of the Munley family and friends as "outright perjury."

He wanted it known for the record that he was the man who had secured the services of the detective. He also wanted it known that he was a son of an Irishman "and I never feel ashamed of it, except when I think of these men as fellow countrymen, men denounced by the church as outcasts from heaven, outcasts of creation and scum of the earth.

"I am a Protestant, although I was partly brought up among Catholics, I have always more than felt that a good Catholic is far, far better than a poor Protestant."

Throughout his address Gowen made references to the detective and insisted that "much honor and glory is due McParlane."

Judge Green instructed the jury with regard to the law on homicide and various degrees of murder. "Now," he said, "you must presume every man is innocent until he is proven guilty. Any reasonable doubt as to the guilt of the prisoner must be in his favor. If you find him guilty of murder, you must determine the degree, such as first, second or manslaughter."

With regard to McParlane's testimony, the Judge said, "If the jury should find that he advised or encouraged the crime with which the prisoner is charged, with a felonious intent to commit the crime that would make him an accomplice in law."

The Judge quickly added, "However, as a detective doing his duty, he would not stand before you as an accomplice and his testimony must be judged and weighed as the testimony of any other witness."

The jury filed back into the courthouse at 4:15 P. M. just forty-five minutes after they left it, and found Munley guilty of murder in the first degree. The jury was polled and each answered, "We find Thomas Munley guilty of murder in the first degree."

Munley's wife ran to him and kissed him, sobbing violently. Passing the jury box, she turned and cried out, "I hope God will punish you men for doing this."

Chapter 7

THE SECOND YOST TRIAL

Aunt Mamie's illness brought the two young lovers together. Marie heard about it outside the church Sunday morning. Aunt Mamie had missed Mass. Marie had heard something about this being a mortal sin, and she knew something was wrong. She hurried to the home of the "witch."

She found Pat Mulrooney in the kitchen with a coffee pot in his hand. She lifted the stove lid with an iron handle and took the coffee pot from Pat.

"Get a bucket of coal from the bin outside," she said. Without a word Pat picked up the scuttle and disappeared. When he returned Marie was upstairs in the bedroom.

She called down, "Put some coal on the fire and open the damper." He did.

Pat started for the stairway but Marie shouted, "Stay down. I'm putting a mustard plaster on her back."

He went back to the kitchen table, sat down and looked over the jumbled notes. He began to put them together in chronological order.

* * * * *

July 14, 1876

The second trial of the Yost murderers opened. The prisoners were Hugh McGeghan, James Carroll, James Roarty and James Boyle. They were on trial for the murder of Frank B. Yost, at Tamaqua on July 6, 1875.

On his deathbed Yost had said he was shot by two men. At the time of the shooting Patrolman Barney McCarron saw two men run up the street and fired at them. One fired back.

McCarron testified they were strangers yet he knew they were all "Irishmen."

In his opening remarks the District Attorney accused McGeghan and Boyle of the actual shooting. Roarty was charged with furnishing the men and a pistol. Carroll was charged with providing the weapons.

Referring to the detective, he said McParlane "came to this region for the purpose of investigating this Order of AOH to discover whether the society was truly a beneficial one or one composed of murderers."

Yost was thirty-three years old when he was shot. His wife saw him on the lamppost ladder from her bedroom window. She ran downstairs and out front where she saw her husband stagger against the garden fence. "Give me a kiss," he cried. "I'm shot and I'm going to die."

He said to Dr. E. S. Soliday, "Doctor, I'm shot in my stomach. This is the last of me. See the blood? I'm vomiting."

Dr. Soliday testified, "I satisfied myself that he was mortally wounded and told him that he had but a short time to live, and that he ought to tell me all he knew about the shooting. Yost told me that he was sure he was the wrong man shot and that they really wanted to shoot Barney McCarron."

The defense objected when James Kerrigan was called to the stand. Submitted in writing, the objection was on the grounds that Kerrigan was a principal in the murder of Yost and because "he is now indicted for the murder of John P. Jones."

The objection was overruled.

Kerrigan swore that Carroll said, "We'll fix Yost and make his head softer than his arm." He testified that McGeghan fired the first shot and Boyle fired next and they both ran. He said he showed them the way.

Kerrigan was asked, "Do you belong to any secret society?"

"We object."

"Overruled."

Kerrigan said, "I joined the AOH and when I got in it I found that it was a society for murdering and burning.

Yellow Jack Donohue put me down on my knees in Alex Campbell's cellar in Tamaqua while Campbell held a candle. Donohue read a prayer and had me kiss the book. We shook hands and I swore I would keep all secrets."

Kerrigan had to memorize the signs, "goods' and passwords because "I can't read or write."

He was asked, "If you knew you had joined a murderous organization why didn't you quit?"

Kerrigan said, "I was afraid I'd get my head knocked in with a lump of lead."

The defense established the fact that Kerrigan was between seventy-five and eighty yards away from the lamp post at the time of the shooting.

Witnesses were heard for the next few days. One was John Churchill who said he knew Kerrigan.

The defense asked, "You can't tell the exact date you met Kerrigan?"

"Yes, I can. It was July 14th or 15th."

The defense continued, "But that doesn't prove that you are sure of the date. Which date was it, the 14th or 15th?"

He answered, "Yes, I am sure of the date, and if you'll take the one day I'll take the other and then we will both be sure."

Barney McCarron, the police officer, said he was with Yost at the Broadway House in Tamaqua between 11:00 P.M. and midnight on July 5 "and we met Kerrigan there."

William H. Evans saw James Boyle on July 6 between 9 and 11:00 A.M. at work. "He was cutting coal at the time."

McParlane the detective, testified he was officially instructed on July 12 or 13, 1875, by Franklin to investigate the killing of Yost. He said he learned on July 17 who the murderers were. He said he got the names from Michael McKenna. "Carroll, however, objected to the shooting that night on account of the policemen being together."

He explained the system of accepting members into the "Irish" organization, its schedule of meetings and method of electing officers.

The detective said, "The obligation I assumed was secret and it seemed all right. Its nature was to promote brotherly love and friendship and to the espousal of each other's cause and it said we should support a brother in all things lawful. There was nothing unlawful or immoral in the constitution or by-laws.

"I violated the obligation the very next day by reporting to Mr. Franklin. I am all Irish."

When McParlane said this, an unidentified elderly woman, obviously Irish, stood up and said, "I can't stand any more of this," and she was promptly escorted from the courtroom.

McParlane continued, "I told the members I was a Catholic, but I never did go to the confessional after I joined, for it would have been sacrilegious. I didn't tell any of the AOH members that I joined to betray them."

(On July 18 the newspapers in the region featured an article on an explosion at the Cameron Colliery. The news release listed Edward Waters and George Wallace as the men caught in the blast and noted that Walters was not expected to recover.)

The defense asked McParlane, "When did Kerrigan first tell you he wanted to kill Jones?"

"July 27th."

"Did he tell you that it was a debt he was to pay?"

"He said it was a debt Tamaqua was to pay."

"Did you tell him you'd help?"

"I did."

"Why didn't you tell him he'd better give it up?"

"I didn't want to have a charge of cowardice preferred against me and perhaps get myself shot."

Captain R. J. Linden, assistant superintendent of the Pinkerton agency, testified that he came to the region in April of 1875 and "I was the means of communication for McParlane."

In opening for the defense, attorney Ryon "urged no prejudices" and insisted the evidence of Kerrigan and McParlane represented "lies under oath." He called Kerrigan a twice-confessed murderer.

He told this story to the jury. "There was a police case in Canada in which a detective brought a man into court and had him convicted. After the man was hanged it was discovered that the detective was one of the murderers in the case."

He ended this story by declaring that "Kerrigan killed Yost with an accomplice or accomplices we do not know."

The defense then presented several character witnesses. Bernard Boyle was one of these and he swore he was with his cousin, James Boyle, until about one o'clock on the morning of the murder. He said he was "blacklisted" prior to the trial. "I also heard that John Mulherrin lost his job because he was a witness at the last trial."

Gowen asked, "Wasn't he discharged because he threatened to burn down the breaker?"

Boyle replied, "I did not hear that."

Mrs. Hannah Boyle, wife of Bernard Boyle, said, "When I heard James was arrested I said that it couldn't be for he was at our house." She called Barney McCarron "a dirty deserter."

Patrick Duffy said he was not a Molly Maguire and knew no secrets. "I was with Kerrigan that night and heard Kerrigan say he would kill Yost when he got a chance."

Gowen asked, "You are a brother of Thomas Duffy?"

Answer, "I am sir."

Gowen, "That is all."

Casper Brell called James Carroll a good neighbor. Herman Marks said Carroll was "always a good neighbor," and Hugh O'Donnell said his wife was at Carroll's home the night of the murder and Carroll was home.

Gowen faced a simple, uneducated man in O'Donnell and questioned the witness concerning the proper time.

"How could you tell the time your wife got home?"

"I told the time my wife came home by the clock!"

"Did you see it or hear it?"

"I heard it strike. It is an eight-day clock and my clock was right."

"Do you tell the time by the striking of the clock or by looking at it?"

"By looking at it."

"What time is it by that clock?" – pointing to the large clock in the courtroom.

"I always tell it when it strikes."

There was loud laughter in the courtroom and O'Donnell stood up. "I'm not going to stand here to be laughed at; that's what I'm telling you." He stepped down and walked out of the courtroom.

There was much hushed talk in the courtroom on July 21 when word spread that William Callahan, a Body Master at

Mahanoy Plane was picked up by police and placed in the Mauch Chunk jail on a charge of perjury in the Alex Campbell case.

That same day it was learned that a true bill was found against Alex Campbell for the murder of B. F. Yost.

July 22

New headlines declared that "the greatest criminal case in the history of the Commonwealth was drawing to a close. The lives of four men hang in the balance."

One added that "General Albright wraps the coils of the rope of fate around the necks of the prisoners."

Ella Breslin, sister of Mrs. Campbell, swore that Campbell was not away from the house that evening.

Mrs. Alex Campbell said McKenna, the detective, stayed overnight at her home. Kerrigan had given her a revolver to keep for him. "It was black and resembles that revolver there."

She was asked, "You know that McGeghan was charged with shooting Yost with that gun?"

She answered, "I heard Kerrigan say so."

The next question followed, "You know at Mauch Chunk that Kerrigan was a witness against your husband?"

She replied, "Yes sir, I seen that he was."

She was questioned further, "Didn't you hear Kerrigan say that this pistol was given to Doyle by your husband to shoot John P. Jones?"

An objection was raised and the question was withdrawn.

Sam Nevine, an outside foreman, said he knew James Boyle and described him as "a quiet man who never caused any disturbances for the five years he worked in the valley."

Sam Pollock said he thought Boyle was "buckshot" and that the AOH and Mollies were the same organization and "its members were all of good character."

Mrs. Yost, the widow, testified. "The night my husband was shot I could see by the light of the lamp that no one followed him down Lehigh Street. I was watching all the time. It would have been impossible for anyone to have followed him without me seeing them."

Several State witnesses said they knew James Carroll as a Mollie and "therefore a man of bad character."

General Albright took the stand. "The organization is a danger to all who inhabit the coal region. Men have been murdered and all sorts of atrocities have been committed through this organization. If a man had a grievance he did not seek redress himself but did so through divisions of this organization. A requisition was made upon some other division and the crime was committed."

He said the testimony of both Kerrigan and McParlane proved this. He reviewed much of the testimony.

"Never was a case presented to a jury in this county that has been surrounded with circumstances of such a peculiar nature as those that surround this case. It is not pretended that James Kerrigan is not as guilty as these prisoners, for he is. He led the men to the murder and away from it. He is of a class that is easily led. Kerrigan was very susceptible. He liked his whiskey."

In his address to the jury, which lasted three hours, General Albright defended the actions of Detective McParlane.

While he was talking, Kate Boyle and Barney Boyle, who had testified on behalf of James Boyle, were arrested for perjury and sent to jail.

July 24, 1876

The Honorable Lin Bartholomew opened for the defense. He began by saying he would "shirk from the danger of convicting an innocent man. And you are to decide the fate of four men, not one of whom is in the full bloom of life.

"The prosecution would have you believe that only the Irish are vile. Putting a thief on the track of a thief makes it difficult to decide which is the bogus jewelry. You must try to distinguish the genuine from the false."

He reminded the jurors that they had nothing to do with public opinion. He then reviewed the actions of the two police officers on the night of the murder.

"As McCarron crossed the railroad tracks he heard two shots and looked around to see his companion with his arms clasping the lamp post in the agonies of death. McCarron pursued the men who committed the deed and, not catching them, he returned to his companion who was making his way home.

"The theory of the prosecution is that Thomas Duffy, indicted separately with these four prisoners, helped plan the murder. They say that for the paltry sum of ten dollars this crime was committed. I will never believe this."

Bartholomew insisted it was "hate that killed Yost and the ten dollars is but a yarn by Kerrigan. The prosecution says Roarty was to engage two men to do the work and that he did procure them and for what? For ten dollars?"

"Ten days later McParlane comes along and tells us that these men told him of their participation in the murder?"

He said Kerrigan gave three different versions of the murder. What was his motive? The greatest reward that can be offered to man – his own life.

"Kerrigan told you he participated in the murder of Jones and that he is also one in the murder of Yost, and so far as I know he has never been indicted for the murder. He confesses to you his guilt, which these four men deny themselves."

He described Kerrigan as a despicable wretch, a curse let loose from Hell, a confessed murderer. He has never been called to the bar of justice for the murder of Jones. He is let loose to feed upon the blood of his fellowmen.

"The court tells you that if a witness falsifies a statement, his whole statement must be disbelieved."

"McParlane knew all the secrets and yet tells you he didn't hear anything for ten days. He transgressed his duties and encouraged crime and took part in it. He never, so far as we know, detected a single crime. He tells you conflicting stories. If you disbelieve one you must do so with all and throw them aside as unworthy of a second thought. His dates and times conflict. He is confused about where, when and who had the guns."

Bartholomew went on to illustrate his point. "Kerrigan tells you he did not take McGeghan and Boyle to the lamppost, but directed Duffy to do this. McParlane tells you that Kerrigan was the man who ordered them to where the murder was committed and away from it."

"McParlane tells you he was a member of the society and knew all its secrets and signs. Why then didn't he go to James Carroll, give him the password and secure the secrets of the Order?"

He said the only evidence against Roarty was the story of Kerrigan about the offer of ten dollars for the murder. "Roarty and Carroll were never placed at the scene of the crime by any of the evidence. They were involved only on evidence offered by Kerrigan and the detective."

The Honorable J. W. Ryon continued for the defense and reminded each man on the jury of the "fearful responsibility taken upon a man when he undertakes, in the name of the law, to deprive a man of his life. It is easy to move public sentiment and I tremble at how the press stimulates public opinion."

He related a celebrated case that centered about a man named James Whelen, who was accused of belonging to a notorious Canadian organization known as "Fenians."

The lawyer said, "There was fearful excitement over the murder of a well known man named D'Arcy McGee. Newspapers pressed fiercely for an arrest. Two detectives said they heard Whelen tell a friend he shot McGee. An ignorant Frenchman swore he saw Whelen shoot the man. Whelen was convicted."

Ryon turned to the judge. "Whelen said 'I am not a Fenian and I am not guilty.' Sentenced to death, he said to the Lord Chief Justice, 'My Lord, even that does not make me guilty' but he was hanged. Later a man named Trotter confessed. It was public sentiment that convicted James Whelen."

Referring to spies and informers, Ryon said, "All here know and admit that Kerrigan is an accomplice. No men of honor, says the law that placed you in the jury box, would associate you with men for the purpose of learning their secrets only to reveal them."

Here he reviewed some of what he termed was conflicting statements from Kerrigan and McParlane. "At one time this detective said policemen were after him in Buffalo and later he said this was untrue. It is hard to decide who is the bigger liar, McKenna or Kerrigan."

"This man Kerrigan tells you he left these four men on the night of July 5 in Carroll's place. A little later a recorder in the County comes in and swears these men weren't there."

"You must believe these four men were either present when Yost was shot or assisted in the commission of the deed up to the last moment, before you can convict them. There is nothing to show that Carroll was there and you might as well leave Roarty out of the case altogether."

The Honorable F. W. Hughes addressed the jury for the Commonwealth. He first made it clear that Thomas Duffy had elected to be tried separately, explaining why there were four prisoners instead of five in court.

Hughes said, "The evidence relative to Thomas Duffy is of no consequence in this case, except insomuch as it may go to prove the guilt of the other four. It is true that James Roarty and James Carroll were not present at the murder, yet they are even more guilty than the actual murderer because they fashioned and molded the murderer. If you are satisfied that McGeghan and Boyle committed the murder and that Roarty and Carroll assisted, they are all equally guilty."

He called the "Molly Maguires another accessory," and argued that the evidence, without that of McParlane and Kerrigan, was sufficient to convict all four men. He asked for a verdict of first degree murder or not guilty, "They are all Molly Maguires, acting under the mask of the AOH."

Hughes reminded the jury that Officer McCarron saw two men but did not know them, yet he does know Kerrigan and Duffy. The defense tells us McGeghan and Boyle went to a ball in Mauch Chunk that night and were seen coming from the dance. "We say they were coming from a murder."

He burst forth at this point with what was described as "a scathing castigation of all Molly Maguires."

With regard to telling lies, Hughes offered an interesting illustration. "I am stopped on the road by a robber who demands my money or my life. I have $500 in my pocket. I hand him $5 and swear that is all I have. I don't think my conscience would be troubled very much."

Hughes insisted that McParlane committed no wrong by discovering the "secrets of these criminals and revealing them. Nor did he violate any obligation. The Molly Maguires must be exterminated."

Judge Pershing told the jurors that "you must find separate verdicts for each of the four defendants."

It was noted, and regarded as rather strange, that no defense lawyer showed up for the verdict. The court appointed Attorney Ramsay Potts.

The Judge asked, "Have you agreed upon a verdict?"

Phil Brememan, foreman replied, "Guilty of murder, in the first degree."

This was repeated for each defendant.

Attorney Potts asked for "an arrest of judgement and time to file my reasons."

Outside it was dark and dismal. A page on the calendar on the wall showed it was Saturday, July 22, 1876.

The clock struck eleven.

Two days later, on Monday, July 24, Alex Campbell was brought into court at Mauch Chunk for a hearing on a new trial.

The defense argued that Campbell was not "at or near" the site of the Jones murder, calling it an insufficient indictment and questioned the testimony of Kerrigan and McParlane. "A man has no right to do evil that good may come."

Court reserved its decision until August 28.

Chapter 8

THE BEGINNING OF THE END

A disheveled, sandy-haired, flushed face appeared in the doorway.

"A stone flight," he called to Pat. "Come on and help me break it up before someone gets hurt."

"Where?" Pat reached for his cap and followed Stan Prokabovich down the pathway outside the Zimmermuth home.

Marie ran down the steps and out the front door, calling from the porch, "Don't go. Don't go."

Stan stopped and looked back. "We've got to try and stop it, Marie. Guys from Raven Run, No. 2 and William Penn are out to beat Lost Creek."

Stone fights were common in the mine patch. Grade school boys gathered jack stones and piled them in thick underbrush. They worked from a shack in the hillsides, called a clubhouse. Pat and Stan knew all about them, having taken part in such disturbances a few years back. Although they took place almost every summer weekend there was seldom anyone badly hurt in the exchange. Boys on one side of the creek spread tales of scoring hits and hearing wild screams, but the reports were never substantiated.

Stan called to Marie; "This looks like a big one. I think we can talk them out of it." Pat and Stan had organized a baseball team and hoped to issue a challenge for "a money game."

Marie watched the run down the dirt road, cut through a church yard and disappear along the railroad tracks. She turned her attention to the roadway just vacated by the two young men. Two small girls were playing hopscotch in blocks formed by a stick on the dirt surface.

Butch Bradigan's boy was showing off with a buzz-saw he made from a button and piece of string. To Marie's ears it sounded like the distant hum of a bumblebee. Mrs.

Flanagan was pushing a pan of dough into a bake oven in the back yard of her home. Old Jake Pretko was pushing a wheelbarrow that held two bags of coal, picked from a nearby culm bank. With clothespins in her mouth, Mrs. McClafferty was leaning out of her back bedroom window, hanging out her wash.

To Marie this was a normal sight and she shrugged her shoulders and went back into the house. She stopped at the table and glanced at Pat's notes. She picked them up carefully and carried them upstairs.

"Who is Stan?" Aunt Mamie was sitting up in bed, propped by pillows.

"He goes to school with Pat and me," Marie said. "Those crazy kids are at it again. It's a wonder the cops don't do something about it. The only thing they do is protect colliery yards." She put Pat's notes on the bed.

"Are you strong enough to go over these? They might take your mind off your pains and aches."

Aunt Mamie was pleased to see that Marie and Pat continued their interest in the Molly Maguire records. She knew something about the idiosyncrasies of youth. They would start some project with a burning passion but soon cast it aside for some new interest. But Pat and Marie were not giving up on the Mollies. She managed a weak smile and nodded.

The temperature on Wednesday, July 26, 1876 was recorded as "ninety in the shade." Thirty-three cells in the Pottsville jail were occupied by ninety-one prisoners. One of them was Michael "Muff" Lawlor, of Shenandoah, who wanted it known he was "no squealer."

Word reached the prison that Ned Curley had killed John Gunning at Centralia. The prisoners weren't as much surprised by the murder as to hear it was being attributed to the Molly Maguires. Ned Curley was looked upon with disdain by the Irish.

Headlines called it the "last" murder by the Mollies. Curley had landed a heavy stone on the back of Gunning's head and the blow was fatal.

Curley had come from Ireland in 1864 and was a director of the poor in the Conyingham District. He also served as deputy tax collector. A diminutive man of five feet inches, he had snake-like eyes, dark chin whiskers and was described as being "selfish, brutal and obstinate."

A deputy coroner named Murphy, a prominent Irishman, was on his way home one night and Curley confronted him with a large pistol, pointed at Murphy's head.

"Pay your taxes," Curley demanded. Murphy produced a receipt, showing the taxes were paid. Curley called it a forgery. Under the circumstances Murphy thought it advisable to "get rid of the highway blackmailer" and he gave Curley twenty dollars.

At a dance a soft-spoken man, watching Curley's disrespectful actions, asked Ned to act like a Christian. Curley pulled out a pistol and shot the man twice in the knee, crippling him for life.

During a commotion on election day Curley shot Martin Welsh in the neck. At Minersville he sneaked up behind a man at a funeral and shot him in the back.

The strange thing about these incidents is that there is no record of Curley serving any time. Although Irish, he was certainly not deserving of any protection on the part of the Molly Maguires.

What prompted the murder of Gunning involved an incident with Curley and Gunning's wife. Curley entered the kitchen in Gunning's home and asked Mrs. Gunning to buy a bucket of huckleberries from him for thirty cents. She refused, and Curley dropped the price to ten cents. After some coaxing she bought them. Just as she was paying Curley, her husband walked into the house.

Gunning inspected the bucket and found it filled with leaves, with a layer of berries on top. He hit Curley on the head with the bucket and pushed him through the front door.

Outside the gate on the pathway outside the home, Gunning's daughter, Margaret, picked up a large stone and hit Curley on the forehead with it. He was badly cut and headed for a doctor's office.

People standing by chided Curley as he passed. One shouted, "Who burned down your house?" Another, "Who collected the $1500 insurance money for a house worth $800?" Others called him names and shouted insults until Curley disappeared into the doctor's office. A home owned by Curley had burned to the ground under "suspicious circumstance."

On his way back home from the doctor's office Curley picked up a rock, ran up behind Gunning and struck him on the head. Gunning died a week later.

At the time Curley was in default of $3,500 in poor district collections. After the incident with Gunning, Curley disappeared. The Centralia Borough Council offered a reward of $200 for his arrest.

The Mollies were accused of hiding Curley. Rumors had it that the Mollies had influence with chief officers in the State. One report noted that M. S. Quay, secretary of the Commonwealth, had paid Jack Kehoe $1000, John J. Slattery $700, and Barney Dolan $500 for their services in defeating Judge Pershing and in helping to elect Governor Hartranft.

Attorney Gowen issued a statement, "I have seen this organization wield a political power in the State which has controlled the election in this great Commonwealth."

For the next few days the notes were compiled and put in chronological order by Marie, with the help of Aunt Mamie, who made her way between the bedroom and kitchen downstairs with the aid of a cane.

There was no word from Pat, and Marie heard from some of her friends that his mother had forbidden him to visit Aunt Mamie's while "that licentious German slut was there to snatch away my son."

Marie was furious and said to Aunt Mamie, "Do the Irish think they are above everybody else? Sure the Mollies were men, but these notes certainly show they were not without guilt. Pat would have us believe the Irish are infallible. I can see there was injustice done to them, but somebody committed these murders."

Aunt Mamie smiled. "Yes, Marie, I've been through these records before. As we proceed, you and Pat are in for some surprises."

This observation prompted Marie to get busy, and with Aunt Mamie's help she began putting the notes in order.

August 8, 1876

On this day eleven Irishmen filed into court in Pottsville, led by John Kehoe, the "King." The others were James Roarty, John Morris, John Gibbons, John Donohue, Michael O'Brien, Dennis F. Canning, Frank McHugh, Chris Donnelly, Thomas Hurley and Michael Doyle.

They were charged with assault and battery with intent to kill William M. Thomas, of Mahanoy City, on June 28, 1875.

(Aunt Mamie touched Marie's arm and stopped her writing.) "This was the beginning of the end for the King, Marie. It took his adversaries a long time, but they got him. There is an old English adage about never crossing a king unless you can eliminate him, and this was done with relentless determination as trial followed trial, conviction after conviction. Many who shared the sunshine of success with him turned on him in the shadows. In spite of an obviously organized effort to dethrone him, it was his Irish friends who sent Jack Kehoe to the gallows."

The move to associate the murders with the Molly Maguires and the efforts to unite the criminal with those who planned the crime continued in each trial.

August 9, 1876

A highlight of the trial on this day centered about Thomas Donohue, a brother of one of the eleven defendants. He was a constable in Butler Township and was to serve a subpoena on four men. He said he couldn't find them.

He was questioned as follows by the prosecution:

Q – "You are a Molly Maguire or a member of the AOH?"

A – "I am not and never was."

Q – "Never?"

A – "I am not."

Q – "Do you swear that you are not?"

A – "I do and I no more killed him than you did."

Throughout this trial the prosecution made it clear that it "does not allege that all three men were present when the crime was committed, but the law says and the court will tell you that if they incited the parties who committed the deed they too are guilty."

It was testified on this day that the Shenandoah division was picked to "do the job" on George Major. John Gibbons, Thomas Hurley, Michael Doyle and the detective were selected. The initial attempt was diverted because "it was not safe with soldiers in town." At least this was the testimony of McKenna.

On June 28, 1875, Thomas was shot outside a mule stable, but he did not die. John Gibbons, Thomas Hurley, Michael Doyle and a youth named John Morris were accused of the shooting.

A break in the solid Irish front was noticed when Frank McHugh, one of the eleven defendants did not sit with the group in court. Bail was furnished for McHugh in the sum of $6,000.

Another highlight of the trial was when Mrs. John Kehoe took the stand. She knew the men and said they traveled from place to place in search of work. She testified that some went as far as Luzerne County and a few even to the State of Illinois. When asked how she knew all this she said in most cases their wives gave her this information.

She was asked if she helped collect money for the defense of the men and Mrs. Kehoe said the collection was to help pay their way while looking for jobs.

Attorney Gowen accused Mrs. Kehoe and Thomas Donohue of "diluting the truth to a very considerable extent."

All eleven men pleaded not guilty to the charge.

When McKenna was asked why he was not with the men the day of the shooting he said he had been sick and John Morris had taken his place. The detective again involved the

Mollies when he swore the attack on Thomas was "done through the organization."

The State attempted to prove the act was planned at a meeting in Mahanoy City. The defense did not deny that the men attended the meeting in question but argued "it was impossible to prove what took place."

The defense asked the jury to decide if McKenna's evidence was sufficient to convict the prisoner. "He contradicted himself. He said he notified the members of the Shenandoah Division of the contemplated murder of Thomas and went there with them. Nothing that he proposed was carried out, but any plan proposed by them was carried out and accomplished without any interference on the part of this man McParlane. He was not at Kehoe's home when he said he was, and the purpose of the meeting was of a different character than that stated by the detective."

The jurors were asked not to rely on the testimony given by Thomas, the man who was shot. "He told many friends he could not identify the men who shot at him and now he tells you he knew perfectly well who some of the men were. Thomas is a convict and a vagrant."

Ten prisoners looked up with astonishment when Frank McHugh took the stand as a witness for the State. He said the meeting was "called by Kehoe for the purpose of killing the two Major brothers and William Thomas."

The reaction in the courtroom was described as an ominous silence. On his return to prison that night Kehoe said to George Beyerie, the warden, "I'm afraid we won't get justice here, but if we don't the 'Old Man' at Harrisburg won't go back on us."

Attorney Garrett, in his opening remarks to the jury for the defense, pointed out that remarks made by McParlane were not corroborated by McHugh. He insisted the characters of the prisoners were good. "The AOH should command your respect as much as the Odd Fellows or Masons. Before McParlane entered the Order there were never any discussions of crime."

He reminded the jurors that several prominent citizens were among those who swore to the good character of the men, particularly Kehoe.

Gowen, in his address for the prosecution, called it "a sure case for the Commonwealth from the start." McHugh was the particular nail that was wanted to close the metaphorical coffin of these prisoners and he came to the course as expected and not a moment to soon.

"His appearance was very much in his favor. He joined the Order under the impression, no doubt, that he was entering a society that would cause his advancement and through which nothing would accrue to him but benefits. He proved that when he discovered that things were not what they seemed; he left it and returned to it no more. The characters of the prisoners were never good."

When Gowen sat down, Attorney L'Velle, for the defense, moved that the jury be discharged, "as Mr. Gowen made allegations without any right, so far as the testimony was concerned." His motion was denied.

Gowen arose again. "The prisoners are cowards who planned the deaths of innocent men but who were too wretchedly cowardly to strike the blow themselves."

Gowen said, "These men can thank God that their bullets did not kill Thomas. If they had gained their objectives this county would soon become a howling wilderness."

"Friendship, unity and Christian charity is the motto of the AOH. Friendship! Why, it is not even a name so far as they are concerned. Unity! Yes, they believe in the unity of death. Christian charity! If this is shooting down men without notice, then they have indulged in it."

"Why was it that Kehoe advocated shooting down those men in broad daylight? Because he considered himself King of Schuylkill County; Kehoe the desperado, the murder, the villain. Let him think of the hundreds of other victims that he has made miserable, and if he has sensibility, if he can think, I do not envy his future life. The only evidence that is put forward to prove his innocence is that he was known among his own people as a Molly Maguire."

In closing he asked the court to "deal gently with Frank McHugh."

Attorney L'Velle again asked the court to discharge the jury. He said Mr. Gowen "spoke of Kehoe, Donnelly and Roarty as murderers, when there was no evidence in the case to prove the allegation."

When this failed the defense presented three points in a move to have the court favor the defendants.

1. "That if McParlane participated in procuring the persons who made the assault as charged, with the knowledge of the fact that such assault was to be made and that no act to prevent it at the time it took place, he is equally guilty of the offense and is an accomplice, even though his intention and purpose may have been to avoid the act."

2. "That McHugh is an accomplice, and as McHugh and McParlane are the only witnesses, the court will advise the jury not to convict on the evidence of accomplices alone."

3. "If McParlane and McHugh are both accomplices their evidence is no stronger that the evidence of one alone would be."

Mr. L'Velle made reference to the Union in his remarks. "I say God bless it, for while it was in existence not one murder was committed. And never was there until wealth began the disintegration of private enterprise. Not one crime was committed in this county before McParlane entered it."

He asked why McParlane did not inform Thomas that his life was in danger. "Instead he makes you a specious and infamous apology. If he were a man would he not try to do his best to save the life of this man, Thomas?

"The prosecution has called these men Molly Maguires, but what these lawyers mean I do not know and I do not believe they know. These prisoners belong to a benevolent society and not a word can be said about this society any more than any other benevolent society."

The prosecution agreed that only two men. "did the deed" but insisted all eleven were involved in a plot to kill Thomas. The expressed objective of the State was to prove "the Order is criminal and the labor union and the Mollies are as far apart as Heaven and Hell."

The jury was out a half-hour. The verdict: "We find the defendants guilty in the manner and form indicated and recommend Frank McHugh to the mercy of the court."

This was on August 14, and the very next day the prisoners were scheduled for trial in a conspiracy to murder William and Jesse Major. The verdict was guilty as charged, except Frank McHugh.

These and subsequent trials for a variety of crimes came up in quick succession. Much of the testimony was repetitious but the notes included some developments that led to convictions through "informers."

It was noted that J. J. Slattery was expelled from the Order for informing the Majors of the plot against them. When Slattery denied the charges he was reinstated in a week. Slattery admitted donating $5 to a fund for the murder of Majors.

Kerrigan admitted he was among those chosen to kill the Majors. He testified that the "Majors had gone home when someone told them they were going to be killed."

Charles Mulherrin complicated things when he said that Slattery was considered "a good man" to kill the Majors. Slattery said his business would not allow him to do this, so he donated the $5 for someone else to do it.

At one of the trials Kerrigan was interrogated:

Q – "You are charged with the murder of John P. Jones?"

A – "Yes sir, and I was with the men the day they did the murder."

Q – "You haven't had your trial yet?"

A – "I guess not or I wouldn't be here."

Q – "When did you find out what kind of an Order you really joined?"

A – "When Slattery gave Alex Campbell $20 to burn down Barney O'Hare's store and when Slattery gave Campbell $15 to get men to go into the school house and beat up O'Hare."

A disagreement at a convention in Tamaqua over who was to get the reward for the slaying of Gomer James on August 14, 1875 came up in the testimony of several witnesses.

Pat Brennan said he was only four or five feet from James when he was murdered "and I saw Thomas Hurley shoot the man."

Q – "Why didn't you tell some of the officers of the law?"

A – "It was a hard crowd there, mostly Irish and I was afraid."

Ben Beacher caught James in his arms as the man fell, but he couldn't swear who did the shooting.

Frank O'Neill swore he wasn't at the Tamaqua convention and Kerrigan swore he saw him there.

McParlane admitted he was on the "committee of arrangements" for a ball to raise money for the defense of Kelly and Doyle. He said, "Sure, I sold fifteen tickets myself."

Pat Brennan, the man who was afraid of the Irish, went through some interesting cross-examination.

Q – "Did you steal a watch from Thomas Lloyd?"

A – "No, sir, I had the privilege of taking his watch and I did take it and gave it back to him in a day."

Q – "Where did you find the watch?"

A – "Hanging on the wall."

Q – "Were you arrested?"

A – 'Not for taking the watch, but for taking a carriage ride."

Q – "How come?"

A – "I stole the horse."

Q – "Did you sell the horse?"

A – "Clarke Dickson sold the horse and gave me $25."

Q – "Did you pass a counterfeit $10 bill on Mrs. Farrell for one dollar's worth of candy?"

A – "The coal company owed me money and gave me a one-dollar bill. I forged it into a ten and got some cigars and candy and $8 change."

Several witnesses swore that Hurley at one time or another after the murder boasted about shooting James. Yet the day after the murder Thomas Williams said he met Pat Brennan. "I asked Brennan who done it and added 'Wasn't it Hurley?' and he said, 'No, it wasn't and what makes you think that?'"

Pat Butler said at the convention that Hurley didn't shoot James. "It was a man named McLean, of Lost Creek, who did it."

The defense argued that if murder was planned on the convention floor "why isn't every delegate in attendance arrested?"

McParlane said the murder was discussed "in committee" and not on the convention floor.

The detective was questioned. "Did you pay money out of the treasury to defend Dougherty, who was charged with the murder of George Major and acquitted?"

McParlane said, "Yes, and I collected some too. I know the man was innocent and I wanted him properly defended."

Q – "Wasn't the money raised for a fire company?"

A – "Yes sir, as I understood it."

Money was paid by the organization as a beneficiary for funerals, for convention dinners and "other incidental expenses."

Pat Dolan, of Big Mine Run, said he was on the committee of grievances at the Tamaqua convention. "I got a piece of paper that directed me to pay Thomas Hurley for services rendered to the Shenandoah division. We threw it out and said the Shenandoah division should pay Hurley. The paper did not say what the services were."

Dolan was questioned as follows:

Q – "Was the complaint about Slattery over giving information to Majors?"

A – "No. It was that he was not of Irish parentage."

Q – "Did you expel Slattery?"

A – "Yes, sir."

Q – "Was there any other business?"

A – "Yes, we expelled another man for bad conduct and still another because he was too much of a politician."

Pat Butler turned informer.

Q – "Do you know of any crimes proposed by leaders of this organization?"

A – "Yes, sir, but the organization doesn't recognize such, but it can't help it."

Q – "Tell us what crimes you know and who committed them."

A – "Well, to start with I committed a crime myself."

Q – "Any others?"

A – Well, Mike McDonough and I went to shoot a man named Burke. We fired at him on his doorstep, but deliberately missed. It was easy to hit him too, because we were almost against the man. It was just as well, for we felt for sure he was so scared he'd leave the country."

Q – "Anything else?"

A – "At a division meeting we were told to go to Muff Lawlor's and there we were told to go to Jackson's to murder a man. Muff played sick. We didn't go and I don't know who the man was we were to kill. Donnelly came to me and showed me Tom Sanger. He wanted me and Pat Shaw to go up in the drift and shoot him but we refused. At one time myself and three others were asked by Boyle to kill Captain Hay and Joseph Reese, but we did not do it. Bucky Donnelly told me he took the men to Raven Run to shoot Sanger."

Q – "What has become of Mike Doyle?"

A – "Kehoe took Doyle to a national convention in New York City and asked for help. He got $100 and Doyle went to the Old Country."

Q – "Is that all?"

A – "Well, at the Tamaqua convention Hurley told me he shot James and at a bar McLean told me he shot James."

August 23, 1876

On this day, seven men went on trial on a charge of aiding and assisting a man to escape punishment for murder. The state alleged that Thomas Hurley killed Gomer James and the seven defendants took part in the conspiracy. The question of being an accessory or an accomplice was argued.

Attorney Ryon, for the defense, told the story. "A judge had a negro servant to whom he became attached because of the faithful manner in which she performed her duties. However, the servant, Sarah, was a runaway slave. The judge learned that the slave hunters were after Sarah and he went to her in the kitchen and gave her $50.

"Sarah,' he said. 'the slave hunters are after you. Take this money and go back to your master.' Sarah went to Canada on the next train. Although the judge told her to return to her owner she knew he didn't mean it. The judge did not want to lay himself open to the charge of helping a fugitive slave to escape."

Attorney Ryon concluded by asking, "Do you say that the Judge was not an accessory?"

Attorney Hughes, for the prosecution, answered: "I don't say anything of the kind. For all purposes and intents, he most certainly was and that is just what I'm trying to prove here. I want to show that you can take part in a conspiracy without being an accessory."

The jury was out fifteen minutes. James Roarty, John Donohue, Patrick Dolan, Christopher Donnelly, Michael O'Brien, Francis O'Neill and Patrick Butler were found "guilty in the manner and form indicated against all the defendants."

Aunt Mamie knew what she was talking about when she said Pat Mulrooney was in for some surprises. She knew at least a half-dozen Irishmen would turn on their fellow men. The late summer and early fall of 1876 proved disastrous to the men from the "Auld Sod."

Arrests. Trials and convictions followed in quick succession. They marked the beginning of the end, not only of the Molly Maguires, but also the AOH.

Aunt Mamie knew that Pat's loyalty and affection for the Irish was to be tested. Pat was in for a surprise that startled even Aunt Mamie,

Charles McAllister went on trial for the murder of Thomas Sanger; John Kehoe faced a charge of accessory before the fact to a murder. Thomas Munley and Charles McAllister were charged with participating in the murder of both Sanger and Uren.

An exchange between Gowen and the governor of the Commonwealth, however, pleased Pat a great deal.

Governor J. F. Hartranft was invited to the dedication of the Soldiers' Cemetery at Summit Hill. The letter also made mention of a rumor that the governor contributed $500 to help pay legal costs for the Molly Maguires.

The governor wrote, "Official engagements preclude my acceptance" in declining the invitation. He continued by calling the $500 rumor "unqualifiedly false, as well as the insinuations made by Mr. Gowen in his recent speech to the jury in one of these trials at Pottsville."

The governor continued, "If Mr. Gowen meant to convey the idea that my action was as an official was in any way influenced by any bargain arrangement, or understanding with anyone, directly or indirectly associated with the society known as the Molly Maguires, then his statement is untrue, and he knows it to be so.

Gowen was in Philadelphia at the time and the *Philadelphia Bulletin* sent a reporter to see the man in the Reading Railroad Company office. After some preliminaries, Gowen read a copy of the Governor's letter and said, "If Governor Hartranft says what I said is not true he is a liar. Give him my compliments."

When the motion for a new trial for Thomas Munley was denied, Judge Green asked the Irishman if he had anything to say.

Munley said, "I haven't much to say, only that I'm as innocent of the crime I am charged with as any man in the world. I never shed any man's blood. I've lived in Gilberton for eleven years and never raised my hand against a man.

Why my life should be sworn away I don't know. That's all I have to say, your honor; only that I'm innocent."

Judge Green said, "Thomas Munley, the sentence of the court is that you be taken to the jail from which you came and from there to a place of execution, and that there you be hanged by the neck until you are dead, dead, dead! And may God in His infinite compassion have mercy on your soul."

Munley replied, "Thank you, Your Honor."

Judge Pershing, in pronouncing sentence on Carroll, Roarty, Boyle and McGeghan said, "Though four of you have been found guilty of murder, only two of you were present. Through the investigation of the case it has been shown that you acted on behalf of an organization that will for long years be regarded with horror."

Carroll had a few words to say, "Your Honor, I've been tried and convicted of a crime of which I am innocent. I'm found guilty on the evidence of two perjured men." He thanked the judge and his defense lawyers for their patience.

James Roarty, "I haven't much to say, Your Honor, only that I am not guilty of what I'm charged with. The public may say I'm as innocent as your Honor and I've no more to say."

James Boyle, "I've nothing to say only I'm innocent of the crime charged and I guess I'm to die for what was done by Kerrigan."

McGeghan, "Nothing at all. I know it would be of no use. I know my life has been sworn away but I hope God will forgive the men who have done it, as I do."

All four were sentenced to be hanged by the neck "until you are dead."

Alex Campbell was brought into court as a principal in the murder of Jones. Judge Dreher and Associate Judges Houston and Wentz occupied the bench.

Judge Dreher announced that the defense filed eight reasons for a new trial and later added five more. He said, "The rule for a new trial is discharged."

Campbell said, "I am innocent of this crime before God and I am willing to suffer for the guilty. There is too much prejudice against me in the courts for me to have a fair trial."

On September 8 Thomas Duffy was on trial for the murder of Yost. He was indicted with James Carroll, James Roarty, James Boyle and Hugh McGeghan but was granted a separate trial.

Meanwhile Mulherrin and Dolan were charged with conspiracy to kill the Major brothers and bail was set at $5,000 for each.

Kerrigan swore under oath that he heard Duffy offer Roarty ten dollars to kill Yost. The lawyers argued about whether a man or an organization was on trial.

On September 21, Thomas Fisher was arrested at Summit Hill as an accessory to the murder of Morgan Powell. A short time later Pat McKenna, of Lansford, was arrested on the same charge.

Powell was shot on December 2, 1871 "by two or three men" and died two days later.

Michael Lawlor was charged with aiding the men who killed Sanger, and in helping them escape.

On September 23 John J. Slattery, John Stanton, Michael Doolan and Charles Mulherrin were arrested on a charge of conspiracy to murder William and Jesse Major. Mulherrin pleaded guilty.

Slattery followed with a confession making a clean breast of his connection with the AOH. He called it a "criminal society" and admitted offering five dollars to save his own life. He warned Mrs. Samuel Major, sister-in-law of Jesse and William, of a plot to kill them.

The jury on the Michael (Muff) Lawlor case did not agree and the jurors were discharged.

John Malloy lived on Little Mountain near Tuscarora and testified that he was a member of the AOH for four years. He said Donahue wanted the Majors shot "but I refused. I wouldn't take any man's life."

Slattery said Campbell had warned him that if he quit the organization he would be shot. "I was told I would be burned alive in me own house."

Mulherrin admitted being at a meeting in Tuscarora "called for the purpose of getting men to kill the Majors." He offered a list of names of men at the meeting.

Michael Doolan and James J. Slattery were found guilty "in the manner and form indicated." John Stanton was found not guilty. Mulherrin had entered a plea of guilt. The court recommended mercy in the case of Slattery. It was Mulherrin who implicated Thomas Fisher and Pat McKenna in the murder of Morgan Powell.

On September 27, Mrs. Hyland, Barney Boyle and Kate Boyle were found guilty of perjury. Edward Monaghan was found guilty as an accessory before the fact in the assault with intent to kill William Thomas. He got seven years.

Thomas Donahue was found guilty of being an accessory after the fact in the assault with intent to kill Thomas. Slattery said Fisher gave Donahue $30 in Malloy's saloon and also gave Mulherrin "a few bucks."

Patrick O'Donnell was arrested for complicity in the murder of Morgan Powell.

Mrs. Kehoe, wife of "the King" was interviewed in her home. She was asked if she knew when her husband would be tried on the various indictments against him.

She said, "I don't know. The court appears to do as it likes about the matter. I presume they will go on with the show as soon as they are ready. When they make up their minds to try a case they try it whether the defense is ready or not.

"I see they convicted the two Boyles and Mrs. Hylan for perjury. If the State thinks perjury should be punished why not arrest Dick Andrews? He swore he saw McAllister shoot Sanger.

"And another thing – that detective McParlane was sitting right there where you are and swore he could not see my kitchen or anyone on the stairway. Now you can see he perjured himself. He also committed perjury when he swore he was here one day that he wasn't."

Mrs. O'Donnell, mother of Mrs. Kehoe, in the room at the time, threw up her head toward the ceiling and said, "The last day will reveal all. Judgment day will decide it. God will not let the innocent suffer in the next world."

Mrs. Kehoe said the value of property had dropped and McAllister's bail was boosted from $2,500 to $4,000.

In a period of one month, eighteen persons were convicted of various crimes and all eighteen were Irish.

John Kehoe, and six other men were found guilty of a conspiracy to kill William Thomas at Mahanoy City. The six men were Chris Donnelly, Dennis F. Canning, Michael O'Brien, Frank McHugh, John Donahue and James Roarty. The trial was over in five days.

Two days later Michael O'Brien, Chris Donnelley, Patrick Dolan, Pat Butler, James Roarty, John Donahue and Frank O'Neill were found guilty of assisting and aiding Thomas Hurley in the murder of Gomer James.

Next came the case against Thomas Duffy. He was accused of being an accessory before the fact in the murder of B. F. Yost. He was found guilty "in the first degree."

James Duffy was found guilty of perjury.

These developments created a mutual distrust of one another among the Irish.

On October 16 fourteen were sentenced. John Kehoe, Dennis Canning, Michael O'Brien and Chris Donnelly got fourteen years. John Morris, John Gibbons and Ed Monaghan all got seven years. Barney Boyle got three years. James Duffy, Kate Boyle and Bridget Hylan got thirty months. Frank O'Neill and Matt Donahue got two years. Pat Dolan Senior got one year.

James Duffy, an aged man, was fined six cents and costs. John Donahue was not sentenced as he was to be tried in Mauch Chunk. Sentence for Slattery, Butler and Mulherrin were postponed at their request.

On October 19 Barney Hayes and John McShea were found guilty of perjury in the Campbell case. They had contradicted McParlane.

Thomas Fisher, Pat McKenna, John Donahue and Alex Campbell were found guilty in the murder of Morgan Powell, although the slaying had remained a mystery for five years.

A mine boss, Powell, went to a store in Summit Hill on December 2, 1871, with Charles, his eighteen-year-old son, the oldest of his five children.

He was shot outside the store by five strange men who disappeared. With his eyes pressed against a store window, the slain man's son saw the strangers but could not identify them. Two men were arrested soon after the shooting but were released for lack of evidence. It was known that Powell had refused Campbell a job in a mine breast and said at the time he would not give Campbell any job where he was boss.

The four men were arrested on testimony offered by Slattery, Mulherrin, Kerrigan and the detective.

The jury, out less than six hours, returned with a verdict of guilty of first-degree murder.

Chapter 9

THE PROSECUTION CONTINUES

Pat was disappointed, but not for long. He was alone in the clubhouse near Fiddler's Green. The boys from the neighborhood had gone home after a downpour ended their stone fight.

Through a paneless window, Pat watched a full moon rise above the tip of a slush bank. Down below on the flat, water trickled through a jagged shallow stream, the overflow from the man-made sandy swimming pool.

At first he couldn't believe so many Irishmen had turned informer. It just couldn't be so; something was wrong with Aunt Mamie's files. Still they had to be authentic, their origin was beyond question.

He was surprised and disappointed. His image of the Irish was severely jolted, yet there had to be an explanation. He was sure there was a reason somewhere for these betrayals, these violations of a trust. Then the thought struck him. What would he do under similar circumstances? Wouldn't he confess to save his life? Yes, that was it. These men saw how well Kerrigan fared out and decided this was the way to escape the hangman's noose. After all only a half-dozen squealed and there were hundreds who stood their ground. A sudden peace came over him when he concluded the informers were the liars.

He took a tablet from the trunk containing the records and placed it on the table. He came upon notes compiled by Aunt Mamie, and although they had nothing to do directly with the Molly Maguire trials they held his interest. They were about an attempted robbery that was attributed to Mollieism. Pat snapped the latch on the trunk and turned to the notes.

* * * * *

Claude White carried a large sum of money on his person. The cash was the payroll for men who worked for him at his colliery.

265

He met two police officers named Clouser and Barnhardt and asked them to accompany him, and they agreed. They drove a wagon along a lonely road at a rapid gait until reaching a spot where the woods grew dense on both sides.

They spotted four men skulking in the trees not far ahead and heard one of them exclaim, "That's our man."

The men came out of the woods and walked toward the wagon. The officers jumped to the ground and turned toward the rear of the wagon. White shouted, "Don't leave me alone."

Barnhardt got back on the wagon seat while Clouser drew his revolver and stood his ground. The four men continued to advance, one ahead of the other three. He saw Clouser's gun and opened fire.

Clouser returned the fire and advanced toward his antagonist, firing as he went. The four men kept coming and the man in the lead was only a few yards away when Clouser took careful aim. Shot through the left shoulder, the bandit fell to the roadway and the other three turned and fled into the woods.

The wounded gunman, Frank Finelly, was placed in the wagon, taken to a doctor in Pottsville, and after treatment was placed in the county prison. He died a week later without revealing the names of his companions.

Soon after this incident White fell from his horse and was seriously injured. He left the mines and opened a neighborhood store in Tamaqua. His fall from the horse was never explained, but it was listed as a mystery.

Clouser, the officer who shot Finelly, was later shot and killed in Hazelton "while in the discharge of his duty."

Barnhardt was later arrested for shooting Pat Hussey in St. Clair. He was tried and acquitted, and soon after left the region.

Pat closed the tablet and mentally noted that although the three gunmen were never identified they were branded as Molly Maguires.

The moon was high now as Pat walked along the banks of Lost Creek. Subconsciously he was drawn toward the narrow wooden bridge that spanned the stream where he first met Marie. The sound of laughter made him look up. He stopped in his tracks when he saw Marie on the bridge with his friend, Stan Prokabovich.

He turned and went directly to the home of Aunt Mamie.

"I'll kill him," he said to the women, after telling her what he saw.

Aunt Mamie was surprised but said nothing for some time. She was sure, however, that Marie's action had something to do with Pat's mother. "After all, Marie has her pride," she figured. "If she wasn't good enough for Pat she had to show she was good enough for others."

"I came across an interesting release on Mike Lawlor," she said, deliberately attempting to take Pat's mind off Stan and Marie. "Perhaps putting this in our script will take your mind off what is bothering you." Suprisingly enough he agreed, and began to make records of court proceedings.

On November 15, 1876, Michael (Muff) Lawlor took the stand in his own behalf. He was charged with being an accessory after the fact in the murder of William Uren, one of the two men killed at Raven Run.

On the morning of the murders he was sitting in his tavern when McParlane and Hurley came in, and Hurley "wondered" how the boys were "getting on" at Raven Run.

He said, "They came in the back door – Doyle first, then James O'Donnell, Charles O'Donnell, James McAllister and Thomas Munley. They got a drink and then told how the murder had been committed. James O'Donnell said he was first to shoot Sanger and then gave another to quiet Uren. O'Donnell said they had made a clean job and they gave their pistols to me. I was about to put them on a shelf when one of them asked me for them and I returned the guns to the men."

"Soon after this my wife came in from a wake she had attended and said she heard some men had been shot at Raven Run."

At this point Lawlor was asked to explain his connection with the AOH. He said he was a member from 1872 to 1874 when "my division dwindled down to two members. I quit and went to Ireland. When I came back I found a new division had been formed in Shenandoah. I went to Kehoe, who gave me a card, and I remained in the division until April first, 1875."

On cross-examination Lawlor said the men had two drinks in his bar that morning.

Q – "Did you drink with them?"

A – "I don't know but what I did."

Q – "How many pistols did you take?"

A – "Two."

Q – "Who gave them to you?"

A – "McParlane."

Q – "The detective. Who owned them?"

A – "I don't know."

Q – "Didn't they exhibit their pistols when they told you how they did the shooting?"

A – "I don't remember."

Q – "You know there was a coroner's inquest held on the bodies of Sanger and Uren?"

A – "Yes, sir."

Q – "Why didn't you attend the inquest?"

A – "I couldn't walk."

Q – "Couldn't you send someone?"

A – "I had no one to send."

Q – "You didn't tell anyone?"

A – "No, sir."

Q – "Didn't you say you knew nothing of the murders?"

A – "I did, and I did so because I was afraid for my life."

Q – "Didn't you call McParlane a perjurer and antichrist?"

A – "I never said he was antichrist because I've read of antichrist and McParlane does not resemble him."

Q – "If you went into the Order for self-protection how is it that you got out of it?"

A – "Because in 1875 I saw that things were going wrong and I wanted to get out of it."

Q – "If you were not a member in September of 1875, how did those men come to you with pistols and tell you all about the murders?"

A - "I don't know, sir."

Q – "Did you ever know of such a thing to occur?"

A – "I didn't know the order was the Molly Maguires until after the arrest of Kelly and Doyle, and I don't know of any other case in which murderers told anyone who was not a member of the order about their crimes."

Lawlor said his home was "fired upon" on a Sunday morning at a time he was away. When asked if he attributed this to the Molly Maguires he said he didn't know.

On the stand Patrick Butler admitted he was a member of the order and was asked if Lawlor was a trusted member. He said, "No, sir."

Q – "Why?"

A – "Because he was looked upon as a coward."

Q – "Do you know of any crime he prevented?"

A – "I know he played off sick when we were to go to Jackson's Mine Patch."

Butler was asked if Lawlor was ever threatened by the organization and the witness said he was, after he sold tickets for a ball and kept the money.

The jury was out for an hour and a half and returned with a verdict of "guilty in the manner and form indicated."

Frank W. S. Langdon, breaker boss at Audenreid, was beaten and stoned on June 14, 1862. He died three days later.

Five years later four Mollies were arrested for the murder. They were John (King) Kehoe, Neil Dougherty,

John Chapman and Michael McGee. Authorities wanted a fifth man, Columbus McGee, but he "left home for foreign shores."

This development was made public on November 24, 1876. On that same day Charles McAllister was found guilty of assault and battery with intent to kill James Riles, of Shenandoah.

Riles was sitting in the doorway of his home at nine-thirty on the night of August 16, 1875 when three men visited him with pistols. Riles got up, and heard a shot and felt a sting in his back. He turned inside and jumped into the garden through a window and climbed over a wooden fence.

A crowd was assembled in front of his home and some were shouting, "Shoot him, shoot him!" One was heard to yell "Turn him out and we'll shoot him."

Riles made his way in the dark to the home of William Kendricks and was later transferred to a hospital in Philadelphia for treatment. When he recovered, Riles sold his home and moved to the state of Illinois. He returned however, to testify during the trial.

Riles said he saw Ned Monaghan and Mike Lawlor that night but "I can't swear to any of the men who fired at me."

William Glover was sitting with Riles at the time and Glover was shot in the arm. He said he could not identify any of the assailants.

Mrs. Margaret O'Donnell swore McAllister was home on the night the shooting took place. Charles McAllister was married to her daughter and Mrs. Kehoe was another daughter of Mrs. O'Donnell. The witness said the accused was "making fuse out of powder and straw for use in the mines at home that night."

Word was received that Mulherrin intended to "squeal."

His trial was postponed and on November 27, Neil Dougherty was put on trial for the murder of F. W. Langdon. The others accused had asked for separate trials.

In his opening remarks for the Commonwealth, General Albright touched on the scene of the murder. He said

Langdon attended a meeting of a group preparing for a Fourth of July celebration. Crowds gathered both inside and outside the hall. Albright said Kehoe "spit on the flag." When Langdon condemned the action he was struck in the face by Kehoe. This followed by other blows with blunt instruments and stones.

Albright said Cyrus Young, in charge of the company store where the meeting was held, "heard stones hit the wall and heard Langdon cry out."

When Young took the stand the defense cross-examined.

Q – "Did you go to the relief of Langdon?"

A – "No, sir."

Q – "Why?"

A – "Because I knew that I would risk my own life by so doing."

Q – "You knew Alex Campbell?"

A – "Yes, sir. I heard the stones strike after Campbell passed out front."

Q – "How was Campbell dressed?"

A – "I don't know, sir. I don't know whether he wore a black or white coat but I do know it was Campbell."

Q – "How many men did you see dressed in white?"

A – "Five or six. Or maybe seven."

James Shearer testified that Dougherty and Kehoe were with him at the hotel when Langdon was beaten.

Charles Augustus Williams, the hotel-keeper, said he nursed Langdon all night and in the morning Langdon refused to ride home and walked from the hotel.

John Chapman said he saw Campbell, Dougherty, Columbus McGee and others drinking in the hotel.

On November 30 the case went to the jury and it was out all night, returning in the morning with a verdict of guilty in the second degree.

It was noted at this time that Lawlor wanted money from Kehoe to finance his defense and he was refused.

December 6

Thomas F. Fisher, and Patrick (Big Pat) McKenna were charged with the murder of Morgan Powell. A similar but separate charge was made against C. T. McHugh. The Commonwealth also considered action on the same charge against Alex Campbell, but since he was already convicted, there was no need to hurry.

A hearing on a request for a new trial for "Yellow Jack Donahue was also scheduled on this date. It was postponed until December 16 after it was rumored he was "going to squeal."

Meanwhile the Commonwealth announced it was reviewing the murder of George K. Smith. The District Attorney declared that "we hope to soon bring the murderers to justice." Smith had been superintendent of Honeybrook Colliery, near Audenreid.

Although no one was accused or arrested, District Attorney Sievers made this published statement. "This horrible and sickening murder was committed by the Molly Maguires, then known as the 'Buckshots.'"

Smith was slain on November 5, 1863, at Audenreid. George W. Ulrich, who later moved to Philadelphia, was a clerk in the colliery office at the time. Ulrich boarded at the Smith home.

Ulrich said Smith returned from Mauch Chunk at 6:30 P.M. on the day he was slain. His clerk told his boss that "something is wrong." He saw men "milling around in the nearby company store." Smith smiled and was quoted as saying, "They won't hurt me."

There was a rap on the front door at 8:00 P. M. Ulrich answered it and thought the visitor was Evan Jones, a Welshman. When the man entered his home Ulrich saw his mistake. The stranger was tall and wore a soldier's overcoat. The visitor asked for Smith. Ulrich said Smith was sick upstairs. The man said he had a letter for Smith.

Ulrich asked for the letter and said he would deliver it, but the man insisted it was a personal matter and he was instructed to deliver it in person. Ulrich called to Mrs. Smith, the former Sarah Troy, who later moved to Mahanoy

City. She came out of the kitchen and went upstairs. A few moments later she called down to wait until the next day.

The visitor said suddenly, "If I can't deliver it to him I must deliver it to you." He put his hand to his back and Ulrich said, "The first thing I saw was the butt end of a Colt revolver. Before he got it out altogether it went off and set his clothes on fire and the ball went down through the floor."

At the sound of the shot Mrs. Smith cried out, "Oh, my God," and Ulrich ran into the next room.

"The tall man caught me around the neck," Ulrich told the District Attorney, "and a smaller man who stepped into the house began beating me on my head and back with a billy. The tall man got out his revolver and put it to the side of my head. I threw up my left hand and the pistol went off and the powder went into my eyes and blinded me for a moment. While this was going on several men came into the room, some disguised as soldiers and others as coal miners.

"They crowded me over against the wall and the tall man tried again to shoot me in the head. I threw up my arms and the pistol ball passed over my head. Then another man fired and the ball went between my legs into the wall. A third man stooped down on his knees and put his pistol to my legs and shot me in the leg.

"I broke away, intending to go upstairs, but they blocked me. At this point Smith came down and walked into the room. I ran into the hallway and they knocked me down and fired two shots over me. I turned around and looked into the room. I saw Smith standing in the crowd and a man came up behind him and put the pistol to his head and fired. Three or four more shots were fired."

The Commonwealth turned its attention to Fisher and McKenna and after the two men pleaded "not guilty" the case opened in the Mauch Chunk court.

Attorney Craig described the murder that took place on December 2, 1871, as an "insidious act by Molly Maguires." He accused Alex Campbell of being the instigator of the murder, declaring that Campbell hated

Powell for not giving him a "breast" in the mine, a place of employment underground. "The murder was perpetrated through Campbell, Fisher, McKenna and their Division," Craig said.

Harry Williamson, the storekeeper, testified that he saw several men outside the store and although he knew Fisher and McKenna, he could not swear they were among the men. He heard one shot, followed by the sound of running feet.

Sam Allen was in the store at the time and on hearing the shot ran out. "Morgan," he said, "who shot you?" Morgan Powell replied weakly that he didn't know. Williamson helped Allen carry Powell into the store. They stretched him on the counter and summoned a doctor.

Michael Meyers swore he saw the crowd and one came up behind him with a gun, but another shouted, "That's not him."

Charles Mulherrin took the stand and said it was understood that Fisher would cough when Powell "leaves the store so he would be known." He said Donahue fired the shot and got $30 in Mulherrin's house for the clean job. He said Fisher paid the money.

Under questioning Mulherrin admitted he knew nothing of any murder plans. He also admitted being tried and convicted of a conspiracy to kill the Major brothers.

Mulherrin, now despised by the defense, was questioned.

Q – "Didn't Captain Linden tell you it would be to your advantage to confess the murder of Powell?"

A – "No, not just in that way."

Q – "Didn't Campbell get a recommendation from someone for a job?"

A – "Yes, he had a note from Father Kelly, and Powell told him to return it to the priest and tell him to go to hell."

Q – "Was Campbell at the store?"

A – "Yes, outside, but he shouted, 'Don't shoot him, he's a friend of mine."

Cornelius T. McHugh testified that there was an argument at a meeting as to whether Jones or Powell should be "put out of the way." He said it was finally agreed to beat up Jones. One of the men was quoted as saying that "Jones might as well put his hands in our pockets and take our money for the way he is docking us on our pay checks." Miners claimed that when the vein of coal "thinned out" both Powell and Jones cut the wages of the worker.

Campbell replaced McHugh as Division Master at the meeting prior to Powell's murder. After this was mentioned by McHugh, the defense claimed that "men will squeal and tell lies and say anything to save themselves."

December 11

Outside the court the streets were white and the blanket thickened as the snowfall grew in intensity. The temperature was down near the zero mark. Someone said the stove "was placed in the courtroom where it would do the least good." The defense insisted McHugh was suspended by the Order "with other squealers" for being drunk and irresponsible. "It is hard to tell what a man will do when you put a rope around his neck."

McHugh was asked if he had talked with his priest about the murder and the witness said he did.

Q – "Didn't you tell your priest that Fisher knew nothing about the murder of Powell?"

A – "My talk with Father Brehony was with a clergyman and not a layman."

Q – "Well, tell us this. Was there a vote taken, to your knowledge, on putting Jones or Powell out of the way?"

A – "No, sir. The organization kept no written records, other than reports on finances."

McHugh couldn't read and did not know why he had been arrested until it was read to him. He was charged with being implicated in the murder of Powell.

Q – "Why did they want to kill Powell?"

A – "Because he was living with another man's wife."

December 12

On this day of the trial Judge Samuel S. Dreher allowed a letter to be admitted in evidence after some argument. It was written by Fisher and was addressed to a friend, A. W. Leisenring. In the communication Fisher points out that "I am not afraid that I have done anything unlawful," but he asked his friend to consult with the District Attorney to see if "he intends to move against me." For his troubles Leisenring was promised Fisher's support in future elections.

December 14

On this day the defense brought Captain Linden to the stand. He was questioned as follows:

Q – "Did you supply Mrs. Mulherrin with the necessities of life and her husband with clothing?"

A – "I did and I didn't."

Q – "Explain that."

A – "I supported Mrs. Mulherrin with the necessities of life, but I gave her husband nothing."

The Commonwealth caused a commotion when Kerrigan, the initial informer, appeared to tell what he had overheard in jail between McKenna and Fisher.

Kerrigan was allowed to testify, and he said Powell was reading a newspaper and said to his friend, "We'll be all right if McHugh does not squeal."

Q – "You are wearing new clothes; how did you get them?"

A – "I had to have new clothes. My old ones wore out showing Molly Maguires the roads to commit murder."

The previous conviction of John Donahue for the murder of Powell was offered and admitted as evidence. The credibility of Mulherrin was challenged by the defense "because this informer would not have confessed if he had not been arrested and placed in jail."

Attorney Ryon, for the defense, termed all informers liars. "when a Molly testifies for a Molly he is telling lies, you say; but when he swears against a Molly he is telling the truth." The lawyer said Mulherrin swore there were a hundred men in the Division when there were only fifteen or twenty members.

John Beyhon testified he was in the crowd at the time of the shooting and swore that Powell said he was shot by Pat Gildea and Pat Breslin.

George Boyle testified that Powell and McKenna were "on good terms as McKenna was driving a gangway, considered a good job, paying $10 per yard."

John Thomas said he saw McKenna across the street through a window while standing on a corner.

Q – "How long did you stand there?"

A – "Ten or fifteen minutes."

Q – "Why?"

A – "Just for pastime."

Q – "You stood on that corner on a cold winter night in December for ten or fifteen minutes just for pastime?"

A – "Yes, sir."

Q – "Where were you born?"

A – "Wales."

Q – "I thought so."

A few other witnesses testified they saw a number of Molly Maguires in the crowd.

William D. Zehner, a mine foreman, was called to the stand.

Q – "Have you discharged men because they were witnesses?"

A – "I may have discharged men who were witnesses but not because they were witnesses."

The defense made it known that Fisher was convicted of assault and battery in 1862. He had appealed the verdict to the State Supreme Court and the county decision was reversed.

Pat Furey testified that he knew Charles Mulherrin "to my own sorrow."

Q – "Why do you say this?"

A – "I never knew a man, woman, or child, English or Irish, Welsh or German, Scotch or American, who said anything good of him."

Q – "What is his reputation for telling the truth?"

A – "It couldn't be worse."

Q – "Did you help raise funds to defend Pat Gildea, who was tried and found not guilty of the murder of Powell?"

A – "Yes, sir. We didn't know what the court might manipulate."

There was a spontaneous roar and he added. "I mean the lawyers."

Pat Breslin was never tried for the murder, as the grand jury had ignored the bill presented.

In his closing address for the Commonwealth, Attorney F. W. Hughes pointed out that a person need not be present where the murder is committed to be guilty. "As long as we prove the accused aided and encouraged the act, he is just as guilty as the actual murderer. Usually a crime is committed by one or two persons but here it is an organized gang, an empire of crime." He recalled that Roarty was not within five miles of where Yost was killed yet he was convicted of murder in the first degree.

In his closing address for the defense, Attorney John W. Ryon called Kerrigan a "lump of blackened iniquity, and Mulherrin is a confirmed liar. Kerrigan has been in jail sixteen months and has not gone on trial yet." He said squealers will say anything to save their own lives. "McKenna is six feet, four inches tall in his boots and Fisher is one of the best known men in the community and yet no one swears they saw either man near Powell that night."

Ryon turned to the twelve men in the jury box and said, "These two accused men will haunt your deathbeds if you find them guilty. Remember – to accept the testimony of

291

Kerrigan, McHugh and Mulherrin, corroboration is needed. What they say must be proven by others to be true."

The jury retired at 3:30 P. M. on December 16 and returned at 7:40 P.M. The twelve men found Fisher guilty of murder in the first degree and McKenna guilty in the second degree.

Two days later the Commonwealth opened its case against Campbell, who was also charged with murder in the slaying of Powell. On this same day "Yellow" Jack Donahue was sentenced. This took place after it was announced that his move for a new trial was denied.

Donahue was asked if he had anything to say. He did. "Your Honor, the men who swore my life away swore it away for money, or to save their own necks. Every one of them swore falsely, Your Honor, but I don't know that talking is going to do my case any good. I have nothing more to say."

He was sentenced to be "taken back to jail and remain there until you are taken to a place of execution where you will be hung by the neck until you are dead, and may God, in His infinite pity, have mercy on your soul."

Campbell's trial was over on December 21 and he was found guilty in the first degree. The jury was out an hour and twenty minutes.

Michael Doyle released a poem he composed in his cell for Christmas. It was published in newspapers of the area at the time, although it was rather lengthy.

The last four lines of the poem makes Doyle's wishes known:

"I will say a word here with hope and cheer,

As Our Lord's birthday is drawing near;

I wish all the best outside and in here,

A Merry Christmas and a Happy New Year."

Chapter 10

FIRE AND FLAME

Pat Mulrooney felt like a man, looked like a man and acted like a man. Since he had gotten the job of patcher on a motor in the Lost Creek mine he became one of the "big guys" in the community. He smoked cigarettes, drank beer and became popular at the "Hoe-down" dances.

Working as a conductor on the bottom lift of the mine developed Pat physically. Muscles bulged in his upper arms, his chest expanded and his legs were sturdy and firm, the shins rippling with becoming symmetrical curves.

Soon after his high school graduation Pat learned there was a job open as door boy. He got his birth certificate from his parish priest and had no difficulty being hired. Mine officials sympathized with Pat since his father had died; his mother was sorely in need of the income.

However, Pat's motive in going to work was not to help at home but to buy a car, clothes and some independence. He made his decision when he saw Marie in a Model T Ford with Prokabovich. If a car was what he needed to win back Marie, a car he would get. Prokabovich used his father's car, but only when he could get it. He would get his own.

Mulrooney was at the kitchen sink removing coal dirt from his face and hands, when the front door opened and Aunt Mamie entered. He could hear the hushed voices of his mother and Mamie but could not make out what they were talking about.

Pat removed a towel from a nearby rack, wiped his hands and face and went into the dining room. Pat's mother and Aunt Mamie were seated at a table with a large open notebook in front of them.

"You two know each other?"

Aunt Mamie looked up. "And why not? We're around much longer than you. We've been keeping up on the Molly Maguire records while you were at work."

Pat said, "Oh, I gave that up."

His mother answered. "Mamie has been showing me your work on this and I find it interesting and believe the job should be finished."

Aunt Mamie quickly convinced Pat "It wouldn't hurt" to look at the notes "while your mother gets your supper ready."

Pat picked up the notes.

Aunt Mamie pointed to the top of a page. "Remember Thomas Fisher, the man arrested for the murder of Morgan Powell? Well, here we come across him in the New Year of 1878. He is described as the living picture of despair in the Mauch Chunk jail. He is waiting word from the Board of Pardons."

Pat read on. Fisher's favorite book was *A Key to Heaven*. He was quoted as saying in an interview at the wicket of his cell, "A man must get used to a thing and after that there is no trouble to bear up under all kinds of adversities."

Friends of Fisher had prepared the petition for the Board of Pardons. It declared Fisher a victim of circumstances. "With a disregard for the evidence the jury convicted the man only because he was a member of the Molly Maguires." The petition appealed for a commutation of the sentence.

What drew Pat's attention however, were notes on Thomas Hurley, who had escaped. Hurley was considered one of the smartest Irishmen in the valley. Pinkerton detectives had been after him since 1875. Here it was three years later and Hurley was still free. At one point in the chase the detectives arrested the wrong man in Illinois. The man was boyish in appearance, had no beard and resembled Hurley, but it was the wrong man.

The detectives traced Hurley to a steamer on the Mississippi. Hurley got word, or at least suspected that men were waiting for him at the next river stop. He jumped overboard, swam to the shore and struck out into the nearby woods.

On January 5 the Ellengowan breaker burned to the ground. It was Saturday night and shoppers in Shenandoah saw the bright light on the eastern horizon. Word got around that it was merely a barn and the shoppers went about their business.

However, a short time later Michael Sullivan, of Lanigan's Patch, rode into the shopping center on a mule and said it was the big breaker. The entire mine village was in danger and 270 colliery jobs were lost.

The cause of the disastrous conflagration was never officially known but authorities attributed it to the Molly Maguires.

Meanwhile Jimmy Kerrigan, the notorious Molly Maguire squealer, had gone to Mexico. He had tried securing work in the anthracite region before this, but was turned away. He did get one job but it lasted only one day. He was stoned by a mob on his way home from work and never went back. Without any luck in Mexico, he returned to the region early in 1878.

Although fearful of hiring Kerrigan, mine officials were known to regard him highly and one said: "Had it not been for Kerrigan, the detective McParlane, would be nowhere."

January 7, 1878

The State Supreme Court reached a decision in the Kehoe case. He had been indicted with others for the murder of Frank W. S. Langdon on June 14, 1862.

The decision was written by Chief Justice Agrew, with Justice Sharwood, Mercur, Gordon, Paxson and Woodworth in agreement. It referred to the case as an atrocious murder. "It may be said here that Kehoe was somewhat intoxicated at the time and by the threats testified were idle bravado, but it by no means follows that he did not mean what he said."

It concluded: "The judgement of the Court of Oyer and Terminer is affirmed and it is ordered that the record be remitted for the purpose of carrying sentence into execution."

This brought Jack Kehoe, Hester, McHugh and Tully to death's door. The Supreme Court had refused to reverse the lower court and unless the Board of Pardons acted, the death sentence was to be executed.

January 8, 1878

It was noted that Dennis "Buckey" Donnelly had been found guilty of murder in the first degree on November 24, 1877, in the death of Thomas Sanger. Now Donnelly's counsel moved for an arrest of judgement and for a new trial. Sanger had been slain on September 1, 1875.

The court denied the motion for a new trial. Donnelly said, "If I got justice from the court and jury the squealers wouldn't swear my life away like this. I'll never forgive them for leaving my poor, weak children without a protector."

Judge Pershing said that of the five men who were present and took part in the murder, but one had thus far been tried, convicted and executed. "You, Donnelly, have been tried and convicted as an accessory before the fact in the killing of Sanger. You were not actually engaged in the murder. You took part in the planning as shown by the evidence. Your reason was that Sanger was discharging Irishmen and filling their places with Englishmen and Cornishmen. In my judgement the evidence against you was conclusive of your guilt."

Donnelly was sentenced to be hanged.

January 12, 1878

Kehoe was described as being depressed in the Pottsville prison. His efforts were bearing no fruit. The "King" was growing thin. His "omnipotent authority among his illiterate associates was gone." He refused to see any visitors outside of his family. He sat on a lonely, desolate throne.

January 14, 1878

Hester, Tully and McHugh were in the Bloomsburg jail. Hester was a bulky, angry man with a good vocabulary. He said that "bigotry is at the bottom of our problem. Men lie under oath. Sure, Buckey Donnelly swore the Mollies met at my home in 1876. I wasn't a member of the order since 1872. At the time we had one meeting at my place and had a fuss with a priest. After that the meetings were held in a rented hall."

Tully told a reporter that "Muff" Lawlor was fired and the company chased him from his home and sold his furniture for back rent.

Tully said that Lawlor then came before the Union and asked for $170 to sue the company for selling his household goods. "I helped him get the money and he left the county with it and went to Shenandoah, where he built a house. Two other men lost their household goods with Lawlor, but "Muff" never gave them a cent."

January 15, 1878

James "Hairy Man" McDonnell was on trial in Mauch Chunk court. Among witnesses who testified against him were Kelly "The Bum," Michael Lawlor, John Slattery and Charles Mulherrin, "all squealers."

That evening a mine explosion at Locustdale killed four men and fatally injured a fifth, with the sixth escaping with what mining men called a miracle. The blast occurred in the west gangway of Potts Colliery, in what was regarded as one of the best ventilated mines in the region.

Walter Dixon was repairing the slope when he heard the cries down below, coming from Joe Kenney, a door boy. Dixon reached Kenney and helped the boy to the surface. Exhausted and horrified, Kenney said the mine wagon in the gangway was riddled, rails twisted and timber smashed.

A rescue team entered the mine and soon came upon the body of George Geiger, a mule driver. One of the men called out, "Is there anyone in there?"

"Yes, for God's sake come and help me out." They found George Shivelhood "a mass of raw flesh." They got him out and continued the search. They soon came upon three other bodies. They were Harry Jones, 50; William Boskett, 45 and in the country only three months; and Hugh Wilson, 55. The mule driver, George Geiger, was 18.

George Shivelhood died sixteen hours after the blast. He talked before he died and said his buddies were victims of after damp. "A feeder was struck in the face of the gangway forcing down the gas, and we were all forced to retreat. Gas can be fired by blowing the light through the gauze of a safety lamp. Boskett blew at his wick and the mine exploded."

The next day a coroner's inquest was held. It concluded that "the explosion was caused by one of the laborers attempting to blow out his safety lamp." And that was the end of that.

January 16, 1878

The Commonwealth did not do too well with the squealers in the James "Hairy Man" McDonnell trial.

James Kerrigan said the man who pointed the pistol at Smith's head and fired was "Humpty" Flynn. "He confessed to me some time ago," Kerrigan said.

Charles Mulherrin testified that Flynn bragged to him about "the clean job on George Smith."

Kelly "The Bum" was in the "Old Country" when Smith was murdered and when he returned to America "learned all about it."

Thomas Durkin and Charles Sharp were arrested with McDonnell and were tried at a later date.

January 17, 1878

True bills were found against "Hairy Man" McDonnell and also against Charles Sharp and Thomas Durkin. At the same time Jack Kehoe and Jack Donahue (deceased) were branded as leaders of the gang.

January 21, 1878

John Kane, of Tuscarora and Michael Birgin, of Girardville, were arrested and charged with the murder of Pat Burns, of Tuscarora.

Although Pinkerton detectives were credited with solving this crime that had occurred almost eight years before this time, it was known that "Hairy Man" talked in jail.

Pat Burns was murdered on Good Friday, April 15, 1870. At the time he was outside boss at the Swamp Colliery, near Tuscarora. He was on his way to work over Dutch Hill when he was hit by two shots fired from the side of the road. Without any other information, authorities immediately concluded and announced that the murder was committed by Molly Maguires.

This was a unique case as although Pat Burns was an Irish Catholic, his wife was English and a Protestant. They had two children who were not baptized in the Catholic Church.

Authorities declared that Kane had conspired with miners to pay extravagant prices for work performed with the money being divided by the men and Kane. Burns knew of this and reported it to company officials. When it was definitely ascertained that Kane was not a Molly Maguire, authorities countered by claiming he was engaged by the Order to perform certain services.

When arrested Kane said he was not a Molly and knew nothing about the murder. "The whole state of Pennsylvania cannot keep me in jail unless they perjure themselves. I'll walk out of here in a day or two."

Michael Birgin said simply that the wrong man was being arrested.

January 24, 1878

Jack Kehoe issued a statement. "There are 80 men at Spring Mountain who know I am innocent, but they are afraid to testify. I had nothing to do with the Langdon murder. There was an awful lot of perjured testimony given during my trial. Slattery perjured his soul while playing the docile witness. He even went so far as to say I got the men who killed my own sister-in-law and brother-in-law. This cut me in the heart. He is steeped in crime and his thoughts of his past life must make him tremble in his squealing boots."

When Mrs. Kehoe learned of this statement she reprimanded her husband for talking to reporters. "Haven't you learned yet that they only want to lie about you?"

Mrs. McDonnell said her husband, "Hairy Man," was drunk the day Burns was killed. "I am sure as I am sitting here that my husband had nothing to do with the murder of George Smith and knows nothing about the Burns murder."

Mrs. Kehoe said: "What does the Commonwealth mean by taking testimony from Kerrigan, Mulherrin and Kelly the

Bum? The Bum and Mulherrin were in Ireland at the time, and Kerrigan was in the Army. Whatever they know is hearsay. It is not right to take that kind of testimony when a man is being tried for his life. There is no justice in it."

January 25, 1878

James McDonnell was brought into court and was asked to identify Michael Birgin. The "Hairy Man" pointed to Birgin and said, "He is the wrong man." Birgin was released. Kane was held for trial.

January 29, 1878

It was announced in Harrisburg that the warrants for the execution of Patrick Hester, Peter McHugh, Patrick Tully, and Jack Kehoe would be issued by the Governor in a few days.

The next day a big boiler at the St. Nicholas Colliery exploded. A fireman, William Kerschner, thirty-six, was killed in the blast, although he was thirty feet away from the explosion.

A coroner's inquest declared that death came by an explosion of a boiler "from causes unknown" but word was out that it was the work of Mollies.

February 2, 1878

It was announced that Kelly "The Bum" was to be indicted and tried for the murder of Alexander Rea. Kelly was flabbergasted. He naturally expected to be liberated. He was further astounded to learn that his testimony during the trials of Hester, Tully and McHugh was to be used against him!

February 6, 1878

The Board of Pardons opened a three-day session in Harrisburg. Mollies were under sentence of death in three counties. Commutation of death sentence to life imprisonment was asked.

In addition the Board was to study thirty-seven new cases and twelve old ones.

February 7, 1878

A postponement was announced in the case of Kelly "The Bum." It was held over to the next term of court. The word was that he was of considerable service in squealing in the case of Thomas Fisher.

Citizens of Columbia County petitioned the Board of Pardons for clemency of at least one of the three men convicted of murdering Rea.

Two specific reasons were given in the plea for mercy for Pat Hester, Peter McHugh or Pat Tully. The first was "because it is a custom and was a custom since earliest times that those invested with the executive power of justice at least would pardon one in a group of criminals." The second was "because we think the Commonwealth and society will be satisfied if one act of mercy replaces actions of severe justice."

February 8, 1878

A letter from Franklin B. Gowen is made public. "The ends of justice would be better served if the case of Manus Coll, alias Kelly 'The Bum' was continued at least to the next term of court." Mr. Gowen was president of the Philadelphia and Reading Coal and Iron Company at the time.

His letter continued. "Squealers should be encouraged. The best way to prevent a reorganized Molly Maguires is to place a premium on squealing. Criminals will be afraid to trust each other. Destroy confidence among conspirators and there will be no more conspiracies."

February 9, 1878

Martin Birgin was arrested near St. Catharine in Canada by Captain Alderson, a coal and iron cop. A Shenandoah citizen had met Birgin and relayed the information to the authorities.

It took the captain three days to secure extradition papers and return Birgin to Pottsville. This time the law was sure it had the right Birgin.

February 14, 1878

Thomas P. Fisher, gave up all hope. He learned that the Board of Pardons had turned him down. His political influence, solicited in many ways during his sixteen months of imprisonment, had failed. He began making a will. He owned the Rising Sun Hotel at Summit Hill.

"A century from now this Mauch Chunk prison will be an historical landmark," he declared. "I am innocent. When the day of my execution comes I will let the public know that I am an innocent man. I will prepare a statement in writing and will get someone to read it. On that Memorial Day I will say that I am innocent of the murder of Morgan Powell. They will believe me then, as I would not be guilty of going into another world with a lie upon my lips. I never entered into any conspiracy either publicly or privately to do any person any harm.

"Through Powell I got a good job driving a counter gangway. Mr. Powell and I were always good friends and I was very sorry when I learned that he was shot. What motive had I to kill him when he favored me in jobs? I was convicted simply because I was a member of the AOH."

Fisher then picked up his copy of *The True Christian*, which explores the mysteries of another world.

February 15, 1878

Dennis Canning said the "minds of Mollies" were being poisoned or prosecution officials were deliberately circulating malicious lies. "Members of Hester's family blame me for inducing Kelly to squeal on Pat Hester. I never saw Kelly in or out of jail and I wouldn't know the Bum if I fell over him."

February 16, 1878

Fisher got a reprieve. He was to hang on February 26. The Governor, on solicitation of Fisher's friends, granted a respite for thirty days, to March 28.

The reason: James Sweeney, of Summit Hill, produced an affidavit which established an alibi for Fisher. He offered proof that Fisher was at Sweeney's saloon when Powell was murdered.

February 23, 1878

John McShea, an inmate in the Mauch Chunk jail, told friends that "Yellow Jack" Donahue said before his execution that Fisher knew nothing about the Powell murder. McShea was in jail because he testified for Campbell and contradicted the testimony of the detective, McParlane. He was sent to jail for perjury.

This same day Governor Hartranft issued the warrants for the executions of Hester, Tully and McHugh. The date set was March 25. He also issued warrants for the execution of John Kehoe and Dennis Donnelly on April 18.

March 4, 1878

Sweeney was warned by prosecution lawyers not to sign his affidavit. They told him his testimony should have been given at the trial and not delayed.

One lawyer was quoted as saying, "Sweeney, if you sign that paper, be the contents true or false, you will be hanged by the neck until you are dead as an accessory to the Powell murder. Nothing but the interference of God above can save you from such a fate and God does not interfere on behalf of Molly Maguires."

Convinced he was in danger, Sweeney finally declared that certain words and meaning were put into the affidavit that were not what he dictated. This was a surprise as Sweeney was far from being illiterate. He was president of the Summit Hill Savings Bank.

Nevertheless, he insisted Fisher was in his saloon, but left for a period of ten or fifteen minutes and returned again, taking a place near the heater. He was there when a boy opened the door abruptly and shouted that Mr. Powell was shot.

The prosecution argued that Fisher could have taken part in the murder during that brief interval. The State went further by announcing plans for the arrest of Sweeney on a charge of perjury.

On this same day the death warrants for John Kehoe and Dennis Donnelly were announced with the date of execution set for April 18. Fisher's execution was set for March 28.

March 6, 1878

Barney Dolan presented the Board of Pardons with a petition containing 2,500 names asking for clemency for three prisoners at Bloomsburg. The petition branded Kelly "The Bum" as a liar in testifying that Hester, Tully and McHugh were at his home in Big Mine Run the day before Rea was shot.

The petitioners declared they were not satisfied with the verdict for three specific reasons:

1. The three men were convicted on the unconfirmed testimony of an accomplice.
2. There was a reasonably well-founded doubt as to the guilt of the condemned.
3. Hester took no part in the commission of the crime. Kelly "The Bum" was a perjurer and was not even in the county when he claimed he was a witness to the murder.

When Dolan returned home he said, "The Board of Pardons would rather pardon the Devil himself than a Molly."

March 13, 1878

It was announced that Fisher would make a public statement on the scaffold on the day of his execution.

March 15, 1878

Martin Birgin arrived at the county jail in Pottsville from Canada.

March 18, 1878

Cornelius T. McHugh, of Summit Hill, turned state's evidence. He said he was selected to take "Yellow Jack" and Mat Donahue from Tamaqua to Summit Hill where they would meet Alex Campbell outside the Burning Mine. He said instead he directed them through the streets of Summit Hill to Sweeney's place so "the crowd could see them and in this way prevent the murder."

March 20, 1878

Hester, Tully and McHugh were doomed. The Board of Pardons decided not to interfere. Hester was astounded. Tully was not surprised: "What is must be." McHugh was resigned, "I guess it is so and can't be helped."

March 21, 1878

Dennis Donnelly's case was placed before the Supreme Court in Philadelphia "on six assignments of errors." The court said the decision would be delayed until the May term of court.

On this day a carpenter went to the prison in Bloomsburg and offered to build three rough boxes for $12. The offer was rejected as being "too cheap."

Chapter 11

THE HANGINGS AT BLOOMSBURG

March 22, 1878

A delegation, led by Mrs. Hester, appealed for a delay of execution on the grounds "these men need more time to prepare for death." Mrs. Hester said, however, that she was consoled by believing she had done all she could for her man. Her friends said Mrs. Hester showed the world she believed in her husband's innocence and fought crushing public prejudice.

Word spread that Tully and McHugh would declare Hester innocent on the scaffold. It reached the governor's office and his private secretary was instructed to be at the execution with a conditional reprieve.

The three prisoners could see the gallows under construction from their cell windows. The scaffold had arrived from Mauch Chunk and rope was purchased for $30.

March 23, 1878

Rumor of a planned rescue spread like wildfire and 150 police officers were assigned to Bloomsburg. Sheriff John W. Hoffman added all county deputies and all available detectives.

Workers assembled twenty-six pieces of seasoned oak. A box of bolts and rods was dumped into the prison yard. Benjamin Franklin, the superintendent of the Pinkerton agency, arrived to supervise the executions.

Hester pronounced "the Irish curse" on anyone who dared see him and declared that Gowen pursued him with "unwarranted vindictiveness."

The jail yard held 75 persons yet 150 passes were issued to detectives, the sheriff's deputies, doctors, priests and newsmen.

All law officers were "on the alert" when Franklin declared: "There are good reasons to believe a rescue will be attempted."

Franklin recalled that during the Donahue trial, back in 1868, for the same Rea murder, the town was twice set on fire.

March 25, 1878

Newspapers reviewed the Rea murder. Hester was tax collector in Mt. Carmel Township and kept a tavern at the time.

It was understood in the saloon that Rea was to carry a payroll of $18,000 on his person the day he was to be slain. Jack Dalton and five other men drank whisky at Hester's bar.

Dalton knew Rea and was to stand on the Water Barrel Road between Centralia and the Coal Ridge Colliery and give a signal by shaking his hat on approach of Rea.

Rea's body was not found until the next day. When murdered he carried only about $50 on his person. He had delivered the payroll the previous day.

Thomas Donahue, John Duffy and Michael Pryor were arrested but released for lack of evidence. Suspicious whispers, however were directed toward Hester. He left the region, but returned in 1869, going to Bloomsburg and surrendering to authorities. He was also discharged for lack of evidence.

Six years later, Kelly "The Bum" was arrested for larceny and at this time implicated Hester in the murder of Rea.

On this same day authorities got a letter from a man living in Peoria, Illinois. The man said he saw the news in a paper on February 28. He notified authorities that he had worked with Hester at the time of the murder and knew Hester was not guilty.

The author of the letter said he was in the wash house when Dan Kelly "told me Hester was in a heap of trouble about the killing of Rea, but had nothing to do with it at all.

Danny said Hester was asked by the group of men to help and he said he wanted that thing stopped. Rea was his friend. Hester asked the men for their revolvers but they refused. He asked them to take a drink and 'we'll hear no more about this.' The plot was carried out without him knowing a thing about it. I write this only to save a man I believe to be innocent."

The letter was sent to the secretary of state and Mrs. Hester received a copy from the man in Illinois.

But the three men hanged on that very day.

March 25, 1878, was a big day in Bloomsburg. Mass was celebrated in the prison that morning, with relatives of the condemned taking part. Tully turned to his wife and said, "Heaven bless you, Bridget."

She whispered, "I have nothing left now but me broken heart."

Carried away by the big event, Bloomsburg took on the atmosphere of a carnival. There was feasting and revelry in practically every bar and poolroom. Stores advertised special sales. There was much pushing and shoving in the streets. Men climbed walls and fences to "take a look." Some men reached the jail roof. Six women somehow got into the prison and peered through the windows of the cells that were occupied by the three condemned men.

Joseph Fry leaned too far out a window in the Exchange Hotel and fell to the street. He died of a crushed skull. A fist fight broke out in one bar and six men required hospital treatment.

A crowd occupied Sheriff Hoffman's woodshed and the roof collapsed. This was a big joke and crowds laughed and cheered. A boy named "Sonny" Williams was on the shed.

When the roof gave way "Sonny" went with it. The boy died of his injuries that night.

Patrick Hester, fifty-two, was a big man, weighing 250 pounds. He had a wife and four daughters.

Patrick Tully, forty-eight, was married to a widow with five children.

Peter McHugh, forty-four was single.

The coffins were carried into the prison yard and dropped to the ground with a bang in full view of the three condemned men. The three men were tied and rope circled their necks. Hideous white caps were placed over their heads.

They said nothing and witnesses said they died game. The trap fell at 11:10 A.M. and the three died together. Hester breathed heavily and every muscle in his large frame worked spasmodically. Faces of spectators turned away in horror.

The bodies were not cut down for thirty minutes. Spectators filling through the prison yard were interrupted by the piercing of a train whistle, pulling into the nearby station. Gowen had arranged for a special train to take the body of Hester back to Locust Gap. The other two bodies were removed by a funeral director from Wilkes-Barre.

At Tully's wake, his wife was told her husband confessed before he was executed. "If he did it was forced on him or just made up by some policeman. Why didn't they say so before he died? It is because he would deny it and can't now."

Hester's gold ring was stolen. His hat and prayer book were missing. Pieces of rope and sections of wood were cut up and taken. Someone removed the white caps from the heads of the three dead men.

March 26, 1878

Fisher refused food delivered to him in his Mauch Chunk cell. He began a fast, which he said was penance for the sins of others. Reading *Preparation for Death* by the light of the small prison window he could see the gallows outside, brought back that day from Bloomsburg.

March 28, 1878

Spreading the fingers and thumb of his right hand, Fisher pressed it against a newly plastered prison wall and declared that the imprint would remain there as a perpetual sign of his innocence.

He turned and walked through the open door, down the corridor, out into the yard, up the improvised stairway and was hanged.

However, Fisher left the statement he promised. It again declared his innocence. He said he was never engaged in any conspiracy, paid no one and was in Sweeney's the evening of the murder, with the exception of the few minutes he went out front.

March 29, 1878

Kelly "The Bum" was imprisoned the day Fisher was executed. Referring to Hester, Tully and McHugh, who were hanged on March 25, Kelly said, "I am sorry now that I was not hanged with the rest of them. I am as guilty as they were. I am sorry my testimony led to the deaths of my friends." He was disowned by his family.

April 2, 1878

A letter written by Pat Hester before his death was made public. It was addressed to Tully and McHugh. He said his friends offered testimony that were lies "and you both know this. I am not guilty and you both know this. I never got up that job or plot."

In the letter Hester said, "I am not afraid to die for I am tired of this sinful world. They are after my life these many years. All that troubles me is to die for what I am not guilty of, and both of you know this. May God have mercy on our souls."

April 3, 1878

Counsel for Dennis Donnelly and Jack Kehoe declared the death warrents were issued after the writ of error was taken to the Supreme Court and were "therefore irregular and not legal." Action on Kehoe's case by the Board of Pardons was set for April 9.

April 6, 1878

The trial of McDonnell, Sharp and Durkin, for the murder of George K. Smith, was set for April 10 at Mauch Chunk.

April 9, 1878

The Board of Pardons met in Harrisburg to hear reasons advanced for the commutation of sentence for Kehoe for the murder of F. W. Langdon, which had taken place sixteen years previously. Affidavits were presented from men in the Eastern Penitentiary, saying Kehoe had nothing to do with the murder. "Yellow Jack" Donahue told his lawyers that he committed the murder, and not Kehoe.

April 11, 1878

James McDonnell went on trial in Mauch Chunk for the murder of George K. Smith. Sharp and Durkin were to be tried at a later date.

April 12, 1878

The majority of the Board of Pardons decided to hold the case of Kehoe over for the quarterly session and instructed the recorder to inform the governor. The Kehoe death warrant was withdrawn by the Governor.

A death warrant was issued to "Buckey" Donnelly with the date of execution listed on May 22.

When Mrs. Kehoe told her husband that his case had been delayed, the King of the Mollies said, "Well, thanks be to God for that much. Maybe when they look more carefully into my case there may be some hope for me yet."

April 13, 1878

Peter McManus and John O'Neill were arrested on a charge of murder. The victim was Frederick Hesser, fifty-five-year-old watchman at the Hickory Mine near Shamokin and a coroner in Northumberland County. His body was found in an old engine house on December 18, 1874. The head was crushed and an arm broken. A hammer and club were found near the body.

April 15, 1878

John Acton of Houtzdale, Clearfield County, was charged with the murder of Frederick Hesser.

Meanwhile, defense attorneys in the Smith murder case insisted squealers were concocting stories against the prisoner. Kerrigan, one of the informers, was described as "an imp of darkness." He was accused of giving wrong dates, offering conflicting fairy tales and of staining his blood with lies.

April 16, 1878

James McDonnell was declared guilty of murder in the first degree. The jury went out at 3:15 P. M. and returned at 7:15 P. M. on April 15. The verdict was announced in regional newspapers on April 16.

The court announced it would use McDonnell as a witness against Martin Birgin and Charles Sharp.

April 19, 1878

The trial of Charles Sharp that began on April 16, was delayed because of the illness of a juror.

April 22, 1878

Charles Sharp was found guilty of murder in the first degree.

The Pottsville court announced the opening of the case against Martin Birgin, John Kehoe and John Brennan for the murder of Pat Burns. Birgin was chosen by the Commonwealth to be tried first.

Three days later he was found guilty of murder in the first degree. The jury was out from 12:30 to 2:20 P. M.

April 29, 1878

It was discovered that one of the jurors on the Dennis "Buckey" Donnelly murder trial was not a citizen. A new trial was requested and denied. The court disposed of this objection in this manner:

"We conceive that there is no substance in this error. The circumstances that disqualify or excuse citizens from serving as jurors are so numerous that it seldom, perhaps never, appears that a panel is drawn without some incompetent name upon it."

May 16, 1878

The Board of Pardons refused to interfere in the Dennis Donnelly execution, set for May 22 in Pottsville.

May 18, 1878

John Kane was set free on a nol-pros entered by the District Attorney.

May 21, 1878

Governor Hartranft issued a respite for Dennis Donnelly for twenty days on application of two priests, acting as spiritual advisors. Father Brennan and Father Gallagher, of St. Patrick's parish in Pottsville, had appealed to the governor to give Donnelly more time to prepare for death.

May 23, 1878

Kelly "The Bum" was released from the Bloomsburg prison on a two-term rule. Arrested in connection with the Rea murder, he was the principal witness against Hester, Tully and McHugh.

Kelly was given a railroad ticket by Sheriff Hoffman. He was the last Molly Maguire to leave the Columbia County Prison.

June 1, 1878

Charles Sharp was convicted of murder in the first degree. He stoutly denied he had anything to do with the murder of Smith. He said "The Bum" told stories that were nothing more than "wicked fiction."

Resigned to his fate, he said, "I will die for the sins of others. I am without friends, money or means of any kind, and since I am not a Mollie I'll get no help from there. My board and store bill was taken out of my last pay before I got it and my balance was nine dollars. I worked every day except Sundays, during the month that Smith was killed."

Sharp left the Molly Maguires in 1873. While a member he had a fistfight with Kelly and kept "The Bum" out of the organization. "Kelly always had a grudge against me. And another thing; Kerrigan swore Alex Campbell gave me an order on Fisher to pay me seven dollars. This is not true. I was the biggest enemy of the gang at Tuscarora."

Sharp said he never spoke to Kerrigan in his life. "I defy anyone to prove I was at the scene of the Smith murder."

He said he was at the home of a relative at the time of the slaying.

June 4, 1878

The Schuylkill County Court overruled a motion for a new trial in the case of Martin Birgin, convicted of first degree murder in the death of Pat Burns.

The execution of Dennis Donnelly was set for June 11. His older brother, John Donnelly, of Raven Run, appeared before the Board of Pardons with an affidavit that impeached the character of Patrick Butler, the chief witness against Donnelly. The Board took no action.

June 7, 1878

The Northumberland County Grand Jury found true bills against McManus and O'Neill, both charged with the murder of Coroner Hesser near Shamokin in 1873. The trials were postponed until the next term of court.

June 8, 1878

Barney Hayes, known as the Irish Orator and in jail for perjury, was released. His parting remark was, "If I had $3,000 I would prosecute Gowen, McParlane and Franklin for murder."

June 11, 1878

Dennis Donnelly was executed in Pottsville as an accessory before the fact in the murder of Thomas P. Sanger. He participated in the Sacrifice of the Mass and received the Sacrament of Confirmation from Bishop Shanahan at the prison.

Witnesses of the execution said Donnelly met death with unfaltering firmness. He was described as having the "personification of gentility." He said nothing and appeared indifferent about his execution.

Guards said he slept well, washed himself when he got up, decorated the cell with a carpet, erected an improvised altar and adorned it with flowers and lighted candles.

His legs were strapped above and below the knees. He walked out into the prison yard between two priests, with a candle in his right hand and a crucifix in his left hand, attached to a chain around his neck. He walked up the steps to the gallows with extraordinary firmness. The two priests chanted the litany for the dying. Officers kept back a crowd of 150 "guests" and kept the narrow pathway open for the awesome procession.

Many winced and drew back when Thomas Waldron, an undertaker, deposited an ice box near the scaffold. Looking straight ahead Donnelly never flinched. He wore a blue coat and vest and dark pants, and his hair was neatly combed. The spectators marveled at his obvious coolness in the face of death.

When asked if he had anything to say he shook his head. At 10:29 A. M. the props were pulled away and the trapdoor opened like a flash.

His brother, who witnesses the execution, said Dennis was proof that the "Mollies were men." He would not implicate others in any crime. He would not lie about the other men. He was calm and peaceful in meeting his Maker.

June 12, 1878

The Board of Pardons announced it would give no further consideration to the case of Jack Kehoe. The appeal was returned to the office of the Governor.

The Governor said he could not interfere with the appeal in any manner and could not pardon Kehoe or commute the sentence without a recommendation from the Board. However, it was noted that he could refuse to sign the death warrant, in which event Kehoe would remain in jail but could be released if a succeeding governor signed it.

June 13, 1878

Thomas Durkin was discharged on a nol-pros entered in his case by the District Attorney. Without any delay Durkin headed for Shanty Patch, near Wilkes-Barre. It was explained that the nol-pros was entered so that the State could try Durkin at anytime in the future, should it see fit to do so.

June 15, 1878

James "Hairy Man" McDonnell argued on a motion for a new trial at Mauch Chunk. His reasons were improper evidence, a verdict against law, some new testimony and that the jury based its verdict on a misapprehension of its duty. He also objected to the charge made by the judge. He said Kerrigan and Mulherrin testified only on what they heard.

It was also announced that the motion for a new trial in the case of Charles Sharp would be argued in another week.

June 22, 1878

Chester N. Farr, private secretary to Governor Hartranft, was interviewed in Pottsville on a trip through the region. The main topic of discussion was John Kehoe. Farr was asked if the Governor was influenced by political pressure.

Farr said that since the Kehoe case was undetermined by the Board of Pardons the death warrant was withdrawn. Kehoe had been found guilty of murder.

"The evidence of two men now undergoing life sentences for the same crime is what convicted Kehoe," the Governor's secretary said. "It is a question as to whether their evidence was legal. They simply testified as to Kehoe having been there about the time of the murder. As to having been an accessory before the fact, the only evidence was that he spit upon the flag, and upon being reprimanded he said he might do worse before the day was over. Langdon was murdered that night. The postponement of Kehoe's hanging had nothing to do with politics and the partisan press is in error in so attributing it."

* * * * *

Pat Mulrooney was slumped over the table, the notes clenched in his hands, when his mother and Aunt Mamie came into the room. His eyes were closed, but he was not asleep. He saw Prokabovich as a heartless mine official. He was refusing Pat a job, keeping him from a livelihood for Marie. He saw himself as a Mollie, ready to fight back.

He looked up suddenly when he saw Aunt Mamie turn at the door and heard her bid his mother goodbye. He got up and followed her down the front steps. He reached her at the gate.

"Have you heard from Marie?"

"Yes, Pat. She comes to my house once in a while."

"Does she ask for me? Is she all right?"

"There is nothing wrong with Marie; it is you, Pat. You are one of those thick Irishmen. Why didn't you answer her invitation to the senior prom? After all, what was she to do when you didn't answer her letter."

"What letter? I never got a letter."

They both looked back toward the house. Aunt Mamie touched him on the shoulder and walked away.

She heard Pat say grimly, under his breath, "A letter! My mother!"

Mulrooney did not go home. He followed Aunt Mamie, overtaking her along the banks of Lost Creek.

"Take me in, will you? I'm not going back there."

Aunt Mamie nodded without saying a word, acting as though she had expected it. They walked in silence to her home.

Mulrooney said the colliery was not scheduled to work the next day and he would therefore not need his working clothes. Before going to bed that night Pat told Aunt Mamie he would "get the rest of my things in the morning when my mother goes to Mass."

Pat spent much of the next day putting the Molly Maguire notes in place.

* * * * *

When the Board of Pardons convened on August 6, 1878, to act on Kehoe's case one of the members was absent. Counsel for Kehoe refused to argue the case without a full board being present.

August 9, 1878

Peter McManus goes on trial, charged with the murder of Fred Hesser. John O'Neill remained in jail, scheduled to be tried on conclusion of the McManus trial.

August 15, 1878

McManus was found guilty of murder in the first degree. Fred Hesser, deputy coroner of Northumberland County, was found murdered in the engine house at the Hickory Swamp Colliery on the morning of December 18, 1874. Hesser had been a member of the Ancient Order of the Knights of the Mystic Chain.

McManus claimed he was convicted on the testimony of Dennis F. Canning, county delegate, who turned squealer. The testimony centered about a conversation McManus and another man, overheard by Canning in the mine. Canning had previously been convicted of a felony and McManus said that Canning would swear that "black is white."

A chart of the mine was produced during the trial and the defense showed that Canning was at least thirty-five feet from the other two men when he claimed he overheard them talk about the Hesser murder.

The first ballot taken by the jury in the McManus case was ten guilty and two not voting. The second was eight guilty and four not voting. The third ballot was six guilty and six not voting. The fourth was eleven for conviction and one not voting. On the fifth ballot all twelve voted guilty in the first degree.

O'Neill was then tried. His mother, a brother, and two sisters swore he was at home all night on the date of the murder.

August 23. 1878

John O'Neill was found guilty of murder in the first degree. It took four ballots. The first eight for conviction and four not guilty. The second was nine to three and the third eleven to one. The fourth was unanimous and O'Neill was convicted.

Defense moved for a new trial for both McManus and O'Neill.

September 5, 1878

After a delay of six months on an application for the commutation of Kehoe's conviction, the Board of Pardons met in Harrisburg.

Counsel for Kehoe argued that their man had been indicted with two others for the Langdon murder. "The same testimony was offered against three prisoners, yet Kehoe was found guilty of murder in the first degree."

The other two had been found guilty in the second degree. Two members of the board, Lear and Latta, voted for commutation. The two others, McCandless and Lynn voted against it.

This meant defeat for Kehoe.

September 12, 1878

McManus and O'Neill were denied the motion for a new trial.

October 9, 1878

McManus was sentenced to death.

October 9, 1878

Gowen called a news conference in Philadelphia on problems dealing with the anthracite industry. Prior to the closing of the parley one of the reporters changed the subject.

Q – "Mr. Gowen, will Jack Kehoe ever hang?"

A – "Certainly."

Q – "They say that a governor elected subsequent to the conviction of a criminal convicted of murder in the first degree never issues a death warrant?"

A – "That used to be a custom before the Board of Pardons was created. Now the responsibility of pardoning is taken from the shoulders of the governor. When the Board refuses to commute or pardon, the governor issues the death warrant."

Q – "He is not compelled to do so?"

A – "Not if he wishes to violate his oath."

With a terse announcement that he had another appointment Mr. Gowen brought the conference to an abrupt close. The reporters filed out, convinced that Kehoe was doomed.

———————————

Marie Swartz unfolded notes she had put aside during the months of research. She leaned forward on the back porch wooden bench outside Aunt Mamie's home. She picked up a pencil that had fallen from her lap and opened a tablet for her notes.

Marie was interested in three particular letters she had uncovered during her search for Molly Maguire records.

The first was a letter to the editor of the *Shenandoah Herald*. She recalled that she had thought it would be of interest to Pat when she had first seen it. Although written poorly it contained evidence of a labor dispute.

She jotted down quotes from the letters.

"Yez keeping publishing the situation of affairs and if yez are fair why the blue blazes don't you tell the public the truth? I will tell yez that the sons-of-bitches of operators and bosses have robbed us out of 30 per cent, instead of 20 per cent. But it took the means of skunks 40 per cent to get it and we intend to make it cost them 40 more to keep it.

"Now, Mr. Editor, that's the true situation. I am against shooting as much as ye are. But the Union is broken up and we have got nothing to defend ourselves with but our revolvers and if we don't use them we shall have to work for 50 cents a day. And I tell yez the other nationalities is the same as we are only they are too dam cowardly. Ye can think and say what yez like; it is all the same to us. But I have told ye the mind of the children of Mistress Molly Maguire."

The second letter that impressed Marie was left behind by James Carroll. In it he thanked the warden, George Beyerie for his kindness, the deputy wardens, Moses Innis and Michael Schoenman; Father McDermott; the Sisters of St. Joseph and the defense attorneys.

Finally he thanked his father, mother, sisters. Brothers and "loving wife."

His letter continued: "Now gentlemen, I do here confess to be innocent of the crime that I am charged with. I never wished for the murder or Mr. Yost or any other person. I never heard anyone say that he would shoot Yost the first chance he got. I never knew Boyle or McGeghan at the time."

"Now gentlemen, you can believe Kerrigan if you choose, but I hope if I have ever wronged any person that they will forgive me as I forgive those who have falsely belied me. I as a dying man, have no animosity toward any person. I hope that there will be no reflection thrown on my friends or family for this." The letter was signed: James Carroll.

The third letter was written by Columbus Roarty, addressed to his condemned son, James Roarty.

Before his execution Roarty said, "I have nothing to say, gentlemen, only that I am innocent of the crime I am charged with. I am going to die innocent. These men who persecuted me and put me to this place, I forgive them from the bottom of my heart. And I hope God will also forgive them."

After receiving Holy Communion from Father McDermott on the morning of his death, Roarty showed the letter from his father.

"Don't be afraid to meet your Judge, Son. If you are going to suffer innocent I am sure God will spare your soul and it is far better to suffer in this world than in the world to come."

"No matter how long we suffer in this cursed world, it is nothing beside eternity. We pray for you night and day."

"Don't be afraid, for God is merciful and good. And before you die declare to your Judge and to the world whether you are guilty or innocent. I do believe your letter saying that you are innocent."

"I hope through the intercession of the Blessed Virgin that you are going to meet with a happy death. I am sure you are. God will have a place prepared for you that will cause you joy and consolation during eternity, and it is not long until I will be with you in the Kingdom of Heaven. So keep yourself stout of heart."

"I wish I was going to eternity along with you; I would be content. Son, I don't know what to say or do, but I will be ever praying for you. And may the Lord of Heaven protect you in your last agony. Goodbye for a while, for I'll shortly be seeing you."

Chapter 12

THE KING IS DEAD

With a silent prayer on his lips, the King of the Mollies toppled from his earthly throne on December 18, 1878.

Jack Kehoe walked firmly to the gallows, turned to his lawyer and priest and said, "I am prepared to die." His last words in response to the Sheriff, were, "I am not guilty of murdering Langdon. I never saw the crime committed."

A blanket of snow covered the prison yard and 200 spectators shivered in the gray, bitter cold morning. The mourners included his grief-stricken wife, parents and six children, as Kehoe paid the supreme penalty for a crime committed over sixteen years before the date of his execution.

It was publicly noted that the day of sorrow for the Irish was a dawn of joy to many colliery officials, and particularly Franklin B. Gowen. The mourning did not stop at the grave, but continued down through the years. It left an indelible mark among the Irish.

(Pat Mulrooney, who was putting these notes together in the parlor of Aunt Mamie's home, had heard just that day, some fifty years after the execution, that the Irish in Girardville were still talking of the detective, McParlane, attacking Kehoe's wife in her home.)

Descendents of Kehoe, and practically all others involved, have yet to believe that the "King" and his Irish subjects were guilty as accused.

They will never believe that trained Irishmen were actually brought into coal fields to cause confusion and dissension, as claimed publicly by Gowen. No one has convinced the Irish that Langdon, as "ticket boss," created animosity only among the Irish. Langdon's job was to "dock" the miner for cars of raw coal containing slate, rock or dirt. Cutting the price was not confined to the Irish. They find it inconceivable to think that only the Irish were sympathetic with the South during the Civil War.

They do believe that Gowen used every means possible to get the Irish to distrust one another. They do believe that he offered rewards for evidence against them, promising pardons and even safe conduct out of the region. Gowen created a central board of coal operators and advocated the discharge of anyone belonging to a labor union. Their names went to this central board and they were "blackballed" at all participating mining operations.

The Molly Maguires were blamed for organized acts of destruction they could not have committed. The 200 men who halted colliery operations at the Forestville Mine could not have all been Mollies.

Dozens of robberies and personal attacks were all blamed on the Mollies, although no one was ever apprehended. Mr. and Mrs. Edwards were beaten and robbed at their home near Pottsville by "ten Irishmen" although no one was ever caught.

The home of Melder Schmidt in New Philadelphia was ransacked on March 2, 1867 by "three Irishmen." The Flour Barrel Tavern was damaged after hours by "five Irishmen" and the home of an aged Ringtown farmer, Henry Rapp, was broken into by "four Irishmen."

In three months the Irish were blamed for five murders, six assaults and twenty-seven robberies.

On June 11, 1869, a mine boss was "beat up" by 200 "Irishmen." How 200 men managed to attack one man is a mystery. That same night Captain P. F. McGinley, an Irishman, was beaten by another gang of "Irishmen."

Gunman fired shots at Amandus Yost in Lost Creek on August 13, 1870. The Irish were blamed because only the Irish lived in Lost Creek. The possibility of someone outside the village coming into the community for the attack was not considered.

The implication was that all starving, desperate men were Irish. Crime waves were the work of the Irish, although it was commonly known that labor and management, in general, were virtually at war.

Facts did not substantiate the widespread claim of Irish influence and domination. Judge James Ryon, supported by his Irish countrymen for reelection to the bench, was defeated by Cyrus L. Pershing, who was drafted by the Republican and "Labor Reform Party of Schuylkill County," although he came from Cambria County.

In an attempt to justify the candidacy of Pershing, Gowen said, "We found it necessary to seek a worthy candidate from outside the county." Pershing had been engaged as a lawyer by the Pennsylvania Railroad for twenty years. Workers pressured by their bosses voted for Pershing, and his election smashed the labor movement in the county.

Political leaders breathed a sigh of relief the day Kehoe was executed with "sealed lips." They were afraid he might talk, Irishmen have said since.

It was labor in general and not the Irish who declared war on "Black Legs" or scabs. It was and still is a principle of labor to brand men who take other men's jobs at lower pay as scabs.

Violence continued almost nightly for almost half of 1875 and all was blamed on the Mollies. A telegraph office was destroyed at Locust Summit, about three dozen coal cars were dumped off the tracks at Locust Gap and engines derailed at Gordon.

Scabbing trainmen were stoned, mules were set free in colliery stables at Shenandoah, and a colliery trestle near Locust Gap was dynamited. A signal tower at Mahanoy Plane was smashed; tools were stolen from colliery carpenter shops and provisions taken from warehouses.

Over a thousand protesting workers, all Mollies, marched through Mahanoy City, and this demonstration brought in government troops.

The Irish never forgot that the detective, McParlane, did not have one man arrested in the act of committing a crime throughout his work in the coal region. They did not forget that the lawyers who defended the Mollies accused McParlane of knowing of planned crimes and allowing them to take place in order to secure convictions.

The Irish believe that the day Kehoe died the Workingmen's Benevolent Association also died.

Mulrooney folded his papers slowly and looked up at Aunt Mamie. She was at the door to the stairway and said simply, "Go out the back way, Pat."

On the porch he came face to face with Marie. Without a word they walked together down the porch steps.

Aunt Mamie watched them from a bedroom window. She smiled when they stopped at the gate, turned toward each other and flushed when their eyes met. Aunt Mamie pulled up a rocking chair.

Through the open window she watched them walk toward the wooden bridge that spanned Lost Creek where they had first kissed. She mumbled to herself. "They are both conscious of a need for each other and love comes from need. She sympathizes with him because he is Irish and he with her because she is not."

The rocking chair moved back and forth, gradually decreasing in velocity, soon coming to a complete stop. The sound in the creaking floorboards grew dim, fading slowly into an eerie silence.

A sharp southeast wind ruffled the large pine trees near the old wooden structure. Marie heard the sound of crackling timber and a sudden gust of wind carried the smell of burning wood to her nostrils.

While racing downstairs she heard the shrieking sound of the siren at the citizen's firehouse. She heard men in the distance shout, "Fire," and on reaching the front porch saw a fire engine race up Duck Street.

She shouted to a group of men scurrying up the winding road. "It's Aunt Mamie's. Pat Mulrooney is there." And in a desperate whisper, "Our Molly records!"

She met Stan Prokabovich on the way and they reached the gate outside the burning building together. They were held back by firemen, and heard a man scream, "There's someone in there."

Marie grabbed Stan's arm. "It's Pat. He's in there. Do something, for God's sake – do something!"

Stan ran along the fence, cut through some wild growth and arrived at the rear of the home in time to see flames burst through the roof. While voices were calling for more hose and better water pressure, he said under his breath, "She asked for Pat. She didn't even mention the witch – only Pat."

Ignoring warnings to "keep back" and "stay put," Stan ran into the home through an open door and stopped in the kitchen. He gasped for breath in the intense heat and fanned at the swirling smoke wildly with his arms, hoping to make out forms in the dark room. He saw no one and in his blind groping stumbled over a solid object. He picked up the large oblong box and threw it through a window, shattering the glass.

A strong, offensive odor of burning hair sickened him and he staggered and grasped the edge of a table for support. Opening his mouth wide in a desperate attempt to breathe, he fell forward as an agonizing pain cut across his chest. He lost consciousness when his body hit the floor with a thud.

In less than a minute two firemen had the prone figure on the grass in the garden. He was carried into a nearby colliery ambulance and was rushed off to Locust Mountain State Hospital.

Marie went from one man to another asking for Pat, and was finally consoled to learn he was in the mine working overtime with a repair crew.

Suddenly Pat's mother appeared at her side. They stared in silence as two firemen carried a body down the front porch stairs on a stretcher. It was covered with a white sheet. Someone shouted, "Back, back, quick." Without a word the two women embraced each other.

Marie looked up when she heard a ruddy-faced boy cry out, "The Witch is dead."

Pat hurried from the mine shaft when he heard the news. He was still wearing his mine cap and lamp when he reached Marie and his mother. The glare of the mine lamp made Mrs. Mulrooney blink. A tall woman, her head was above Marie's, whose back was turned to Pat. The older woman wiped a moist brow with a shawl. Marie sobbed bitterly, her face pressed against Mrs. Mulrooney's breast. Drawn together by a mutual affection for Aunt Mamie and sharing an instinctive compassion in this tragic moment, the two women remained locked in a consoling embrace.

An overwhelming grief filled the hearts of the two women, casting off deep-rooted prejudicial barriers. Dumfounded for a moment, Pat's amazement was quickly transformed into an inner sense of satisfaction, an engrossing, profound joy.

Marie turned and ran into Pat's arms. "Oh God, Pat." She cried, "Aunt Mamie is gone." Nothing was said for what seemed like an eternity to Pat and then Marie stepped back and exclaimed: "The Molly Maguire records!"

One of the firemen returning from the blazing home overheard Marie and stopped. "Your records are safe. They were in a trunk that Prokabovich threw through a window."

The next day Pat and Marie spent some time with Stan at the hospital. Propped high on his bed, Stan watched them walk down the corridor and muttered under his breath: "I wonder if I could have done it if I knew what was in that trunk?"

Chapter 13
THE FINAL WORD

The Miner's Journal Volume 1, Number 7, published on June 4th 1877 in Pottsville shouted at the reader with the headline: MOLLIE MAGUIRES BROUGHT TO JUSTICE AT LAST. The subtitle summarized: 1) *Fourteen years of crime in PA,* 2) *Numerous murders committed since 1862, and* 3) *Murderers to be hanged Thursday, June 21st.*

The paper included a statement by the editor and an article addressed to the people by Franklin Gowen. At this time they were both biased toward the coal company. Mr. Gowen expressed his relief that "the labor unions have been erratically dissolved" and the "secret association of Molly Maguires has been broken up." The fourteen years ending in 1876 were terrorized with robbery, assault, attempted murders, and other outrages including "12 brutal assassinations of prominent citizens."

No mention is made of the unsolved crimes, especially the murder of the son and daughter of Charles O'Donnell in Wiggans, near Shenandoah, on the night of December 10, 1875. The crime has never been solved.

Franklin B. Gowen was the president of the Reading Company. He was a District Attorney in Schuylkill County during the Civil War period. Early in the 1870s the Reading Company was threatened by the expansion of the Pennsylvania and Lehigh Valley Railroads into the coal fields of Schuylkill County. The area was a prime location for the railroads' expansion. The papers were also predicting that the Jersey Central Railroad would be coming into Schuylkill County.

There were six anthracite corporations functioning throughout the hard coal regions of Northeastern Pennsylvania but only one was denied the right to own coal lands, Gowen's Reading Company.

Franklin Gowen using his persuasive and convincing oratory manipulated the members of the state senate and congress to get the right to own coal mines. Despite several failures of incorporating the Franklin Coal Company to own and operate coal mines, he finally succeeded by disguising the bill. During a debate by the legislature members of the Senate realized that the Reading Coal Company was behind the bill. The proposed corporation, Laurel Run Improvement Company, was voted down 17 to 15 in the morning session. Gowen proceeded to work a miracle during the lunch break by using his articulate conversation and flair for entertainment on a group of senators.

Three of the bill's opponents were absent and one other changed his mind when they returned from lunch. The measure passed by a comfortable margin. Now the Reading Company monopoly could begin but first Gowen would have to secure the coal land and remove the "irresponsible trade union."

Franklin Gowen used the Laurel Run Improvement Company to buy 70,000 acres of coal lands. The company changed to the Pennsylvania and Reading Coal and Iron (P&R C&I) in December 1871. The P&R C&I would continue to buy coal land until they owned 100,000 acres.

Gowen told the company stockholders that the Reading Company had secured and attached "a body of coal land capable of supplying all the coal tonnage that can possibly be transported over the road for centuries." He could now turn his efforts to dissolve the labor unions.

The major events that happened in the fourteen years from 1862 through 1876 as they occurred in chronological order are listed in Table 1.

Despite all of the efforts by Franklin B. Gowen the P&R C&I had an astounding total operating loss of $12,257,568 for the period from1876 to 1887. In 1888, Gowen reported, that the monies needed to restore efficient operating procedure to the mines cost the company $1,186,614. The company went into bankruptcy and Gowen was fired as its president. On December 14, 1889, Franklin B. Gowen committed suicide in a hotel in Washington, D. C.

The trials of the "Molly Maguires" were a travesty of justice. It is a time of embarrassment for the judicial system in the history of our country. The trials were conducted with open hostility against Irish Catholics. The judge in Jack

Table 1. Chronology of major events in the 14 years between 1862 & 1876.

June 14, 1862	Audenreid	Frank Langdon, a ticket boss is murdered. He is beaten to death by 5 men.
Nov. 5, 1863	Audenreid	George K. Smith is murdered. He owned and operated a mine.
Jan. 10, 1866	Pottsville	The first of five murders in the County in 1866 started with Henry Dunne, a mine supervisor. He is murdered (shot) by 5 gunmen.
Mar. 15, 1867	Glen Carbon	William Littlehales, Superintendent at the Glen Carbon Coal Company is shot to death. His eyes were shot out.
Mar. 23, 1867	Zion Grove	Henry Johnson was murdered by a half-dozen men.
Oct. 17, 1868	Mt. Carmel	Alexander Rea is murdered, but it appears to be a payroll robbery attempt.
Apr. 15, 1870	Tuscarora	Patrick Burns, a mine foreman was murdered.
Nov. 1870	Schuylkill County	Mr. Gowen is elected President of the P&RC&I. He is 26 years old when he is elected District Attorney.
Dec. 2, 1871	Summit Hill	Morgan Powell is murdered
1872	Shamokin	The Frank B. Gowen Colliery is burned to the ground and Mr. J. J. Green of Centralia has both his ears cut off. An outspoken school teacher, he opposed all the violence.
Oct. 27, 1873	Chicago	Pat McParlane at 29 years of age is hired as a detective by the Pinkerton Detective Agency in Chicago.
February 1874	Shenandoah	Pat McParlane arrived in Shenandoah.
Oct. 30, 1874	Mahanoy City	During a free-for-all George Major, the Chief Burgess of Mahanoy City is shot and killed.
Dec. 18, 1874	Shamokin	Fred Hesser, a night watchmen at the Hickory Swamp colliery near Shamokin, clubbed to death.
1875	Centralia	(During the first 6 mths) In Centralia, Michael Lunation and Thomas Dougherty are shot to

		death. The exact date of the murder is missing.
June 1875	Schuylkill & Carbon County	The "Long Strike" ended with the miners accepting a 20 percent cut in wages.
July 6, 1875	Tamaqua	Benjamin Yost, the Chief of Police, is shot.
Aug. 14, 1875	Lansford	Gomer James is shot by 1 gunman.
Aug. 14, 1875	Girardville	Thomas Gayther, a Justice of the Peace, is murdered by an enraged man (possibly while on a killing spree.)
Sept. 1, 1875	Raven Run	Thomas Sanger, an inside mine boss, and William Uren, a miner, were murdered.
Sept. 3, 1875	Lansford	John P. Jones is murdered.
Dec. 10, 1875	Wiggans	A son and daughter of Charles O'Donnell were murdered. They were shot by about 50 men. There were about a half dozen bullets in each body. The crime was never solved.
Jan. 1, 1876	Mauch Chunk	James Kerrigan was indicted for the murder of John J. Jones. This was the first of the many Molly Trials to be recorded.
May 4, 1876	Pottsville	The Yost Murder Trial begins for five Molly Maguires.
June 22, 1876	Mauch Chunk	The Alex Campbell trial started.
May 5, 1876	Shenandoah	John Kehoe is arrested for assault and battery with the intent to kill.
Nov. 24, 1876	Pottsville	Charles McAllister was hanged for the murder of James Riles.

Kehoe's trial was an old political enemy. Judge Pershing did not allow key witnesses to testify. Irish and Catholic alike were not allowed to serve on any of the juries.

The prosecution was conducted by Franklin B. Gowen and General John Albright, a mine operator's attorney. The

369

General wore his full military regalia to emphasize his patriotism.

The evidence against the accused men was provided by the Pinkerton Detective Agency spy, McParlane. His testimony was corroborated by men who were granted immunity for their own crimes. James Kerrigan confessed to one murder and then retracted his confession, but his wife testified that Kerrigan did commit the murder that he was accusing others of committing while he himself was on trial.

Witnesses testifying for the accused miners were indicted for perjury. Several of these witnesses were women and all those accused of perjury were sentenced to thirty months in the county prison. This made many of the defense's witnesses reluctant to testify, even for their close friends.

The bizarre way the trials were conducted and the speed in which they were pushed through the courts are very troubling to current legal experts. The rush by the jurors and the guidance and direction of the courts show that a miscarriage of justice happened near the end of the century. The judicial system appeared to be corrupt. It abandoned its responsibility and turned the courtroom over to the coal company allowing it to take the law into its own hands.

The coal company used a private police force to arrest the men; hand picked the juries, put fear into the minds of potential witnesses and provided the gallows and the hangman. It was a time when the coal region experienced lawlessness on both sides of the courtroom. This does not justify murder but the question was always there. How many innocent men were convicted and sentenced to die? All this was done in an effort to subdue labor movements and attempt to make the rich coal fields throughout several counties available for personal gain of one man and his company.

Table 2 shows the expediency with which the Molly Maguires were prosecuted once the process got started with their arrests. There were five unsolved murders in the three counties at the time McParlane came on the scene in Shenandoah in February of 1874. After he came on the scene, seven more murders were committed. Crimes unsolved for twelve years were suddenly resolved in less than two as soon as James Kerrigan confessed to the murder of John P. Jones. He decided to accept the Prosecution's promise of freedom by pointing to men who helped to convict others for the 1868 murder of Alexander Rea.

The squealer started to point at men that he either had a run-in with in his past or with whom he appeared to have a problem. Soon other men started to point at someone feeling that it would be possible to save their own lives. In eighteen months forty-one men were arrested, tried and convicted; each a participant in some criminal act.

Table 3 shows that the sentencing varied, from 1 year to the death penalty. Twenty-five of the men were hanged. Five of the men were released with time served for being a state witness. Gowen requested the court to show mercy for the five witnesses. One individual escaped while awaiting a retrial. His first trial, which took a jury 15 minutes to decide, found him guilty of murder as charged.

TABLE 2. The key dates associated with the twenty-five Molly Maguires sentenced to hang.

MOLLY	CRIME	ARRESTED	TRIAL	SENTENCE	NOTES
Charles McAllister	8/16/1875	2/10/1876	6/23/1876	11/24/1876	Hanged for the James Riles Murder
James Boyle	7/6/1875	2/4/1876	5/4/1876	6/21/1877	Hanged in Pottsville for Chief Benjamin Yost Murder
James Carroll	7/6/1875	2/4/1876	5/4/1876	6/21/1877	Hanged in Pottsville for Chief Benjamin Yost Murder
Thomas Duffy	7/6/1875	2/4/1876	5/4/1876	6/21/1877	Hanged in Pottsville for Chief Benjamin Yost Murder
Hugh McGeghan	7/6/1875	2/4/1876	5/4/1876	6/21/1877	Hanged in Pottsville for Chief Benjamin Yost Murder
James Roarty	8/14/1875	2/4/1876	8/23/1876	6/21/1877	Hanged in Pottsville for Gomer Jones & Chief B. Yost Murders
Thomas Munley	9/1/1875	2/10/1876	6/26/1876	6/21/1877	Hanged in Pottsville for Thomas Sanger (& Uren) Murder
James Doyle	9/3/1875	Jan/1876	3/28/1876	6/21/1877	Hanged in Mauch Chunk for the murder of John P. Jones
Edward Kelly	9/3/1875	Jan/1876	3/28/1876	6/21/1877	Hanged in Mauch Chunk for the murder of John P. Jones
Patrick Hester	10/17/1868	3/25/1877	1/7/1878	3/25/1878	Hanged in Bloomsburg for the murder of Alexander Rea
Peter McHugh	10/17/1868	3/25/1877	1/7/1878	3/25/1878	Hanged in Bloomsburg for the murder of Alexander Rea
Patrick Tully	10/17/1868	3/25/1877	1/7/1878	3/25/1878	Hanged in Bloomsburg for the murder of Alexander Rea
Alex Campbell	12/2/1871	4/13/1876	6/21/1877	3/28/1878	Hanged in Mauch Chunk for the murder of Morgan Powell
John (Yellow Jack) Donahue	12/2/1871	2/4/1876	6/21/1877	3/28/1878	Hanged in Mauch Chunk for the murder of Morgan Powell
Thomas Fisher	12/2/1871	9/21/1877	12/16/1877	3/28/1878	Hanged in Mauch Chunk for the murder of Morgan Powell
Patrick McKenna	12/2/1871	10/19/1876	12/16/1877	3/28/1878	Hanged in Mauch Chunk for the murder of Morgan Powell
Patrick O'Donnell	12/2/1871	9/27/1876	12/16/1877	3/28/1878	Hanged in Mauch Chunk for the murder of Morgan Powell
Dennis (Buckey) Donnelly	9/1/1875	11/24/1877	1/8/1878	6/11/1878	Hanged for the murder of Thomas Sanger
John "Black Jack" Kehoe	6/14/1862	5/5/1875	8/23/1876	12/18/1878	Hanged in Pottsville for the murder of Frank WS. Langdon
James (Hairy) McDonnell	4/15/1870	2/9/1878	4/16/1878	1/15/1879	Hanged in Mauch Chunk for the murder of George K. Smith
Charles Sharpe	4/15/1870	2/9/1878	4/22/1878	1/15/1879	Hanged in Mauch Chunk for the murder of Pat Burns
Martin Bergen (Birgin)	12/18/1874	2/9/1878	4/22/1878	1/16/1879	Hanged in Pottsville for the murder of Pat Burns
John O'Neill	12/18/1874	4/13/1878	8/23/1878	3/25/1879	Hanged for the murder of Frederick Hesser
Peter McManus	12/18/1874	4/13/1878	8/9/1878	10/9/1879	Hanged in Sunbury for the murder of Frederick Hesser
Thomas Hurley	8/14/1875	8/8/1876	8/23/1876	(12/18/78)	Jury took 15 min to convict for the murder of Gomer Jones – (Escaped)

Reviewing the Pinkerton Detective Agency archives of McParlane's career showed that a similar incident was prevented in a responsible judicial system. McParlane was promoted to chief of the Pinkerton Denver division. He was hired by the state of Idaho to find the murderers of Ex-Governor Frank Steurenberg. The accuseds were arrested in Denver, kidnapped, and taken to Boise, Idaho. They were charged with the murder of Frank Steurenberg.

During the trial, a state witness confessed to the murder and stated that he was influenced by McParlane to turn state's evidence. The defense attorney, Clarence Darrow, showed that McParlane had used the witness in exactly the same manner as he had used Kerrigan in the Molly Maguire cases. Darrow's cross-examination revealed that the witness was coached by McParlane. When the Pinkerton Detective Agency reports were made public in the Idaho Historical Society they fully confirmed Darrow's charges.

McParlane described the link between the Molly Maguire case to the plan to pin Steurenberg's murder on the leaders of the Western Federation of Miners.

McParlane declared: "I cited to Orchard cases in which the state witnesses went entirely free, and to put the matter more forcibly to him and to bring it home to the personal side of the present case, I cited and named personally the Molly Maguire state witnesses who saved their own necks....."

The mass movement in the defense of the accused in Idaho was instrumental in securing their freedom. Unfortunately, no such movement existed at the time of the Molly Maguire trials and it has taken more than a century for justice to be done.

The history of the hanging events and the sentencing summary of several others illustrated in the previous tables beg the question: How many of these people were innocent but found guilty by association?

The trials were found to be a farce and it took a hundred years to finally convince the government. Statements made by the President Judge of Carbon County, John P. Lavelle, and a member of the White House Counsel, Robert S.

TABLE 3. The summary of dates with those that were either released or guilty to a lesser degree.

MOLLY	CRIME	ARRESTED	TRIAL	SENTENCE	NOTES
John Kane	4/15/1870	1/21/1878	4/22/1878	None	Set Free nol-pros in the murder of Pat Burns 5/18/1878
Thomas Donahue	6/28/1875	Dec. 1876		9/27/1876	Accessory after the fact - murder of William Thomas
Frank McHugh	6/28/1875	8/8/1876	8/9/1876	Mercy of Court	State Witness. Mercy of the court 10/16/1876
Cornelius T. McHugh	6/28/1875	None	None	None	State Witness - no charges
Francis (Frank) O'Neill	6/28/1875	2/4/1876	8/23/1876	10/16/1876	2 years as an accessory in the murder of William Thomas
Matt Donohue	6/28/1875	2/4/1876	8/23/1876	10/16/1876	2 years as an accessory in the murder of William Thomas
John Gibbons	6/28/1875	Feb. 1876	9/27/1876	10/16/1876	7 years as an accessory in the murder of William Thomas
Edward Monaghan	6/28/1875	Feb. 1876	9/27/1876	10/16/1876	7 years as an accessory in the murder of William Thomas
John Morris	6/28/1875	Feb. 1876	9/27/1876	10/16/1876	7 years as an accessory in the murder of William Thomas
Barney Boyle	6/28/1875	2/4/1876	8/23/1876	10/16/1876	3 Years accessory in the murder of Gomer Jones
Patrick Butler	6/28/1875	Feb. 1876	8/23/1876	10/16/1876	1 Year Assisting Thomas Hurley in the murder of Gomer Jones
Patrick Dolan Sr.	6/28/1875	Feb. 1876	8/23/1876	10/16/1876	1 Year Assisting Thomas Hurley in the murder of Gomer Jones
Chris Donnelly	6/28/1875	2/4/1876	8/23/1876	10/16/1876	10 years as an accessory in the William Thomas murder
Michael O'Brien	8/14/1875	2/4/1876	8/23/1876	10/16/1876	14 Years accessory in the murder of Gomer Jones
Dennis Canning	8/14/1875	Feb. 1876	8/23/1876	10/16/1876	14 Years - conspiracy to murder William Thomas
Kate Boyle	Aug. 1876	Aug. 1876	Oct. 1876	10/16/1876	30 months for perjury
James Duffy	Aug. 1876	Aug. 1876	Oct. 1876	10/16/1876	6 cents and court costs
Bridget Hylan	Aug. 1876	Aug. 1876	Oct. 1876	10/16/1876	30 months for perjury
James Kerrigan	9/3/1875	3/27/1876	5/12/1876	Time Served	Turned free in 19 months, even after a confession July 1877
Manus (Kelly the Bum) Coll	5/5/1876	2/2/1878	2/8/1878	Time Served Pardoned	Admitted killing Alexander Rea, turned states evidence, never indicted

Bennett, a Partner Skadden, ARPS, approximately one hundred years later, indicated that there was wide spread discrimination of the Irish in North Eastern Pennsylvania accompanied with greed and corruption in the judicial process indicated that a gross miscarriage of justice occurred. So that history would not repeat itself these times should be studied carefully to prevent such injustice from occurring again in our country.

The efforts of Gene Salay of the Pennsylvania State Historical Society, Jim Brennan a representative of the State Labor History Society, Attorney John Elliott, Philadelphia and Joseph Wayne, of Girardville, the great grandson of Kehoe, have reached a closure for one part of the story. Appeals to have other Molly Maguires pardoned posthumously are planned by their descendents. The effort described in Chapter 14, The Epilogue, will continue for the remaining Irishmen. The recent deaths of Attorney John Elliott and Jim Brennan have slowed the process down but the Irish Molly descendants will continue the process where they left off.

Chapter 14

THE EPILOGUE

Some 75 years after the curtain fell on "The Valley of Fear" a strange man entered the Hibernian House at Girardville; the place once owned and operated by "Black Jack Kehoe."

October 1953

The stranger held the door ajar for a moment so all inside could hear the shrill cackle of the geese overhead. In a soft undertone the stranger said; "Going south a bit early I'd say. The winter ahead I suppose."

The few patrons at the bar said nothing.

The visitor turned his attention to a man sitting at a table against the wall opposite the bar. The wall was embellished with replicas of Irish antiques and historical sites and scenes of Ireland.

The man at the table reminded the visitor of "an oversized leprechaun." The seated man wore a bright green jacket, with collar high, touching a profusion of graying hair that fell over his ears. Dark, freshly pressed pants came to an end an inch above his ankles.

All in the room turned when the visitor announced: "I am Friday O'Donnell."

The man at the table said, "So what!"

Patrons of the Hibernian House retained the skepticism of their ancestors when the subject came up, especially when voiced by a stranger.

Historical records list two persons shot to death in the O'Donnell-McAllister home at Wiggans some 75 years ago. Charles O'Donnell and Ellen O'Donnell McAllister were slain. Mrs. McAllister was 20 years of age and pregnant. James (Friday) O'Donnell, brother of the two victims, was not at home at the time.

The man at the table said, "How can you be Friday O'Donnell?"

The visitor answered, "You've read about the man who escaped at Wiggans seventy-five years ago. I am his son."

The beer in the glasses on the bar was now flat. All eyes were on the stranger. The seated man asked for some identification. The stranger placed a driver's license on the table. The man at the table stood up. He said, "The name on this card is Jack Devers."

The visitor responded quickly, "I know. I know. But can I tell my story?"

One man at the bar said: "Go ahead, but wait until we have a fresh beer."

The man now known as Jack Devers ordered a beer. He sat on the edge of the table, his right leg dangling above the floor.

The story he told, "James (Friday) O'Donnell was on his way home that night when he heard the shots from a pathway at the rear of the home. Screams from inside the building pierced the stimulating night air.

"Spurred to action by an instinctive fear, in frenzied haste he sped through underbrush and lightly used dirt pathways. He heard footsteps coming from the general direction of the house and a few moments later sounds of rifle and pistol shots. He pulled up out of breath and whispered a prayer of gratitude as the moon disappeared in dark, dense clouds.

"A train whistle drew his attention and he turned toward the St. Nicholas railroad yards. He came upon "trips" of cars on side tracks, filled with coal.

"He heard steam coming from the engine coupled to freight cars. It was moving slowly eastward out of the yard. Friday leaped to the bottom step on the caboose and stumbled to the floor inside.

"The train was picking up speed before Friday lifted his eyes. He found himself staring at two high-buttoned shoes. He raised his head and looked into the eyes of a brakeman.

"With sudden despair Friday made the sign of the cross. The brakeman responded immediately: "Amen, Brother,

Amen." It was one of the signs and passwords used by the Mollies."

The visitor paused to sip his beer.

A man at the bar said: "What you say sounds good, but you could have read it somewhere. What about your name Jack Devers?"

"Let me continue. The freight train, now in full swing, passed through Mahanoy Tunnel and went on eastward. The brakeman asked for a name. Friday O'Donnell's mother's maiden name was Devers, so he said Jack Devers."

Going from one freight train to another the man now called Devers made his way into New York City. He worked as a common labor on various jobs, "fell in love, married, and here I am, Friday's son."

The man seated at the table was the first to react. He stood up, extended his right arm and said, "I do believe you." All at the bar followed and after shaking hands the drinks were "on the house."

When the visitor departed some time later that night the man at the table followed. He touched the visitor on the right shoulder and said: "I am the son of Pat and Marie Mulrooney."

Without a word he turned away from the visitor. He adjusted the collar of his jacket and the visitor gazed wide-eyed at a Roman collar.

January 1979

John "Black Jack" Kehoe, king of the Molly Maguires, was granted a pardon, one hundred years after he was hanged.

Kehoe was executed in Pottsville, Schuylkill County, Pennsylvania, on December 18, 1878. From June 21, 1877 to October 9, 1879 some twenty Irishmen hanged.

A full pardon, issued and dated January 12, 1979, was signed by Milton J. Shapp, while serving as Governor of Pennsylvania, (See Figure 1, A copy of the Pardon). Barton A. Fields, Secretary of the Commonwealth, also signed it.

Action by relatives and friends of Kehoe brought about the posthumous pardon. Attorney John Elliott, Philadelphia and representatives of the State Labor History Society joined Joseph Wayne, great grandson of Kehoe, of Girardville, the hometown of "Black Jack" in the unique action.

Ernest Kline, then Lieutenant Governor and Chairman of the Pardon Board presented the memorandum in support of the application for the pardon. The work of an exhaustive research, the memorandum carried a compelling summation.

Powerful Points in the Memorandum

A. Religious, social and ethnic bigotry overwhelmingly evident in the trial.

B. A jury that excluded Irish-American ancestry and Roman Catholics. Manipulated a jury from nearby Lebanon County into Schuylkill County, all members unable to speak English.

C. Having coal mining witnesses fired, blacklisted, evicted and barred from company owned stores.

D. Kehoe imprisoned without bail was thrust into a primitive dungeon, with coal company police serving as jailers. This was an outright violation of the Sixth and Eighth Amendments.

E. Franklin B. Gowen, coal company president, served as prosecutor and was aided by General Charles Albright, who appeared in full military regalia.

F. Judge Cyrus Pershing, in charge, was a business and political associate of Prosecutor Gowen and was brought from Cambia County for the trial.

G. Judge Cyrus Pershing was known for his anti-Catholic and anti-labor backgrounds. As a legislator he voted against the 13th Amendment and the Emancipation Proclamation.

H. Pershing, sitting as Judge, violated the Canons of Judicial Responsibility.

POSTHUMOUS PARDON

Commonwealth of Pennsylvania

Governor's Office

To all to whom these Presents shall come, Greeting:

Whereas, At a Court of Over and Terminer in and for the County of Schuylkill held at Pottsville in said County at No. 1269 July Sessions, A.D. one thousand eight hundred and seventy-six a certain JOHN KEHOE was convicted upon a certain Indictment charging him with the crime of Murder in the First Degree

and was by the said Court on the 16th day of April A.D. one thousand eight hundred and seventy-seven thereupon sentenced him to pay a fine of -- to the Commonwealth, the costs of prosecution and Death by Hanging (Executed December 18, 1878)

And Whereas, The Board of Pardons, after full hearing, upon due public notice, and in open session, have recommended to me, in writing, with the reasons therefor, at length, the pardon of the said JOHN KEHOE, which recommendation and reasons have been filed in the office of the Lieutenant Governor.

Therefore, Know Ye, That in consideration of the premises and by virtue of the authority vested in me by the Constitution, I have pardoned the said JOHN KEHOE of the crime whereof he was convicted as aforesaid, and he is hereby thereof fully pardoned accordingly. (Posthumously)

Given under my hand and the Great Seal of the State, at the City of Harrisburg, this 12th day of January in the year of our Lord one thousand nine hundred and seventy-nine

By the Governor: Milton J. Shapp
Governor of Pennsylvania

Barton A. Fields
Secretary of the Commonwealth

Figure 1. The Posthumous Pardon of John "Black Jack" Kehoe.

Other arguments included inflammatory statements by Judge Pershing: A "rancid, slanted press;" no eyewitnesses and Kehoe never placed near the scenes of the alleged crime.

Documents by university historians noted that Gowen spent four million dollars to break the labor union. The same source noted that the State Pardon Board deadlocked with a two-to-two vote to free Kehoe. Defense attorneys never got the testimony from the Captain of the Pinkerton Agency to whom John Donahue had declared Kehoe innocent. Gowen and the Agency simply made the Captain unavailable and Kehoe was hanged.

It was Joseph Wayne who undertook the monumental task of securing and assembling testimony that convinced Commonwealth authorities of a century old grave miscarriage of justice.

Wayne's dogged, persevering determination succeeded in the unique endeavor. A scrappy public figure, Wayne's positions included County Controller, an auditor for the State, a special assistant to a Commonwealth official and president of the Girardville Borough Council. He secured the able assistance of Attorneys John and Thomas Elliott, of Philadelphia. The lawyers were not only Irish but their "roots" were in the Anthracite Region.

Wayne worked out his "pardon plans" at the Hibernian House in Girardville, the very site that served as "Black Jack's" headquarters. It was Wayne who broke the silence in "The Valley of Fear."

For many years after the trials and hangings, the Irish in the region remained hushed and "in hiding" with children and grandchildren, warned of mentioning the subject.

The region became known as "The Valley of Fear" as relatives of those hanged lived with the uneasy feeling of being arrested. There was the constant threatening danger of some ardent fanatic company official or an "informer' wanting to "make a name" for himself with influential authorities. An ominous silence spread through the coal land and lingered down through the years.

An inscription on a grave in St. Jerome's Cemetery in Tamaqua: "Jack Kehoe, a native of County Wicklow,

Ireland, died Dec. 18, 1878, aged 41 years, five months and 15 days. May his soul rest in peace, Amen. Whilst in the silent grave I sleep. Erected by beloved wife Mary A. Kehoe."

The following inscription was added seven years after the original: "Mary Ann Kehoe. Died in August 1885, aged 37 years. May her soul rest in peace."

Although Gene C. Salay lives in Bethlehem, 60 miles east of Molly Maguire country, he is a student of the century old saga. He is an active member of the Jack Kehoe Division of the Ancient Order of Hibernians (AOH). Some years ago he vowed that if Kehoe is pardoned he will seek the same for the others who were hanged. However only nine of the executions took place in Schuylkill County. The proof of "miscarriage of justice" would have to be proven in three counties outside of Schuylkill.

Salay hopes to succeed with the help of the Pennsylvania State Historical Society.

And Joe Wayne.

GLOSSARY

After damp	a gas not fit for breathing, remaining after an explosion of fire damp in mines; it is formed in the explosion of fire damp in mines, and is hence called after damp; it is also know as choke damp, and mephitic air. it is produced in the fermentation of liquors, and by the combustion and decomposition of organic substances, or other substances containing carbon.
Black Legs	a miner regarded as contemptible because they would either be hired to replace a striking worker or continue to work while others were on strike. They would not join a labor union.
Blacklisted	a list of miners or organizations that have incurred disapproval or suspicion or are to be boycotted or otherwise penalized, for some reason thought deserving of censure or punishment;
Bobtail	pay checks which could only be cashed at a company owned store and most often that had the amount cut short to take out costs for items used in the mine.
Body Master	one appointed or elected to preside over an organized body of people, such as an assembly or a meeting.
Braitch	the face of a mine or tunnel, most often attributed to an abandoned coal mine tunnel.
Breaker	specifically: a machine for breaking rocks, or for breaking coal at the mines; also, the building in which such a machine is placed, that is, a building used to process the newly mined anthracite coal by breaking it up.
Breast	mining of coal is done by a system of pillars and breasts. A mine breast is a chamber driven two or three hundred feet at right angles to the airway which is parallel to the gangway
Buncombe	flattering talk for a selfish purpose; empty or insincere talk said for mere show, generally speech-making to gain public sympathy.

Buckshots	an early name given to the organization attributed to the violence in the coal country until the violence was finally associated with the Molly Maguires.
Coalbank	a hill made up of coal or coal byproducts.
Coalhole	a coal mine, usually abandoned or an illegal mine opening. It is often used when referring to a bin used for temporary holding coal
Colliery	a coal mine and its collected buildings (breaker, wash house, etc.), the place where the coal is dug; processed and prepared for shipment.
Culm	the waste from anthracite coal mines, consisting of fine coal, coal dust, dirt, rock sandstones, shales, limestones, and conglomerates.
Cutting coal	an excavation or cut through a vein of coal by digging or probing using mine tools sometimes referred as robbing a pillar, i.e, taking coal from the support section of the mine.
Dinky bank	the slang name for a pile of mine waste, usually slate and other unusable rock.
Docking	to withhold or deduct a part from one's wages for various reasons such as equipment used to do the job, unauthorized absences or to deprive a miner of a benefit, especially as a punishment.
Door boy	open and shut the door as men and cars pass through the door, which controls and regulates the ventilation of the mine. Not a laborious job but very monotonous.
Drift	to pile up in banks or heaps of rock, dirt, culm, or debris, usually transported and deposited by workers or heaped up by currents of air or water.
Feeder	a small lateral lode falling into the main coal vein or a worker or the device that feeds materials into a machine for further processing. It is also used to describe a strong discharge of gas from a fissure often called a blower.
Fenians	a legendary group of heroic Irish warriors of the second and third centuries A.D. which continued later a membership of a secret revolutionary organization in the United States and Ireland in the mid-19th century, dedicated to the overthrow of British rule in Ireland.

391

Gangway	the main highway of a mine. It is a permanent heavily timbered passage or way into or out of the mine with mine car tracks, single or double used by tne miners to travel to and from their working places and it is also a part of the ventilation system.
Goonie	a large rock suitable for throwing.
Grog Mills	the local establishment providing an alcoholic liquor, especially rum diluted with water.
Huckleberries	glossy, blackish, many-seeded edible fruit of New World shrubs or bushes found in the anthracite coal mining region, often called blueberries.
Lode	a deposit of coal occurring within definite boundaries between clearly demarcated layers of rock.
Lokey	a small steam locomotive that was used to move coal cars and sometimes passengers between mining operations.
Parlor	a room for less formal use, in a private home or at an inn or a tavern affording limited privacy where visitors are received and entertained.
Patcher	the person responsible to mend, repair, or put together, especially fast, clumsily, or poorly to connect mis-functioning equipment temporarily.
Patches	small communities outside of a certified town or village or a small piece, part or section, especially that which differs from or contrasts with the whole town or village.
Pluck Me	company stores, owned and operated by the mine owners
Pole line	the right-of-way where the electric lines run through the wooded area.
Powder House	the storage building for the explosive mixture used in gunnery, blasting, etc.; Such as, gunpowder or some other explosive used for blasting in mine shafts.
Shanty (shandy)	a small shed, roughly built, often a ramshackle cabin or shack, a mean dwelling or a rough, slight building or a hut for temporary use.

Slush Bank	a dump comprised of mining byproducts usually from the breakers made up of soft mud, slop or mire.
Starter	person responsible for starting the internal-combustion engine without hand cranking
Sticker bushes	a thorn, prickle, barb or brier bush.
Thinned out	taking the support away from its primary use, such as the lumber, rock, or coal used to brace a shaft, gangway, or any specific opening.
Ticket Boss	the man responsible for assigning a miner to a particular job or task.
Wash house	the facility where the miners could clean up after their shift was finished.
Wicket	a small gate or door that is part of the larger cell door through which business can be transacted.

BIBLIOGRAPHY

The Miner's Journal, Volume 1, Number 7, June 4, 1877-+

The Shenandoah Evening Herald 19th Century Archives

The Pottsville (PA) Republican & Evening Herald 20th Century Archives

The Philadelphia Inquirer 19th Century Archives.

The Molly Maguires, The Origin, Growth, and Character of the Organization, F. P. Dewees, A Member of the Schuylkill County Bar, J. B. Lippincott & Co., 1877.

Lament for the Molly Maguires, Arthur H. Lewis, Harcourt, Brace & World, Inc., 1964.

The Overthrow of the Molly Maguires, Stories from the Archives of the Pinkerton Detective Agency, Cleveland Moffett, McClure's Magazine, 1894, pp. 90 – 100.

Tales of the Mine Country, Eric McKeever, 1992.

The Molly Maguires, Anthony Bimba, International PublishersCo., Inc., 1982.

The Land of the Black Diamonds, Stanley E. Sluzakis, Vantage Press Inc., 1969.

The Legend of the Molly Maguires Video Tape, The History Channel, 1980.

The Mollies Were Men, Tom Barrett, First Edition, Vantage Press Inc., 1969.

Anthracite Coal Mines and Mining, Rosamond D. Rhone, The American Monthly Review of Reviews, November, 1902.

About the Author

Dr. Barrett was born in Shenandoah in 1938 and he learned very early from his dad to plan on getting away from the mines. After his father passed away, he found all of his father's original notes and research material, he tracked additional information from the Internet and old newspaper files. The new records and the attraction of the Molly Maguire legend made Tom want to complete the story.

Dr. Barrett, working as an analyst and system engineer, learned to keep accurate evidence and notes. He used this experience and talent to integrate and edit the original version of *The Mollies Were Men* to create this second edition as *The Final Chapter* giving closure to this violent era.

Printed in the United States
1064300001B